BERLITZ®

OXFORD and STRATFORD

1988/1989 Edition

By the staff of Berlitz Guides
A Macmillan Company

4th Printing
1989/1990 Edition

How to use our guide

- All the practical information, hints and tips that you will need before and during the trip start on page 100.

- For general background, see the sections The Region and the People, p. 6, and A Brief History, p. 12.

- All the sights to see are listed between pages 22 and 81. Our own choice of sights most highly recommended is pinpointed by the Berlitz traveller symbol.

- Entertainment, sports, shopping and leisure activities are described between pages 81 and 91, while information on restaurants and cuisine is to be found on pages 92 to 99.

- Finally, there is an index at the back of the book, pp. 127–128.

Although we make every effort to ensure the accuracy of all the information in this book, changes occur incessantly. We cannot therefore take responsibility for facts, prices, addresses and circumstances in general that are constantly subject to alteration. Our guides are updated on a regular basis as we reprint, and we are always grateful to readers who let us know of any errors, changes or serious omissions they come across.

Text: Tom Brosnahan
Photography: Erling Mandelmann
Layout: Aude Aquoise
We are particularly grateful to Sheila Allen and Philip Willison for their help in the preparation of this guide. We would like also to extend our thanks for their kind collaboration to the British Tourist Authority.
Cartography: 🅕 Falk-Verlag, Hamburg.

Contents

The Region and the People		6
A Brief History		12
Where to Go		22
	Oxford	24
	Oxford Environs	40
	Stratford-upon-Avon	48
	Shakespeare Country	59
	The Cotswolds	66
What to Do	Shopping	81
	Sports	84
	Nightlife	89
	Calendar of Events	90
Dining and Drinks		92
Blueprint for a Perfect Trip (Practical Information)		100
Index		127

Maps

The Heart of England	9
Oxford	25
Stratford-upon-Avon	49
Shakespeare Country	59
The Cotswolds	67

The Region and the People

Few places have been so closely identified with a man as Stratford-upon-Avon with William Shakespeare. The birthplace of England's greatest poet and playwright stands at the centre of what has come to be known as Shakespeare Country. This is "English England"—a robust yet gentle land of half-timbered houses, squat Norman churches and cosy villages.

The area has no strict geographical limits; only a mood, a style and an atmosphere give it unity. The pleasant rolling countryside eventually merges with the Cotswold Hills, dotted with sheep farms and grey stone villages. And beyond it lies Oxford, a "capital" of learning and academic achievement. The whole forms a region best described as the "heart of England"—a world

away from London's bustle, but as close as a train ticket and an hour's ride.

Leave London's Paddington Station after breakfast, and tour Oxford before a late lunch. By tea time you'll be getting to know Stratford-upon-Avon. The triangle bounded roughly by Oxford, Stratford and the Cotswold city of Cheltenham—not much larger than Greater London itself—is surprisingly easy to visit by car, train or bus, by bicycle or on foot. Whether you spend a day or a week, you'll have paid a revealing visit to the English at home.

In the country, the rituals of English life are still observed: tea and scones at four o'clock, muddy walks in rubber boots, the weekly market-day. Country people aren't strangers to modernity, but they reject the

The best of both worlds: town and country meet in English heartland.

frenetic pace of London. No wonder. The romance of English history is all around them, and it's up to them to keep it alive.

Every age has left its mark here. Bronze Age man erected the monolithic Rollright Stones, near the Cotswold village of Little Compton, at the same time as Egyptian workmen were building the pyramids. Roman conquerors laid arrow-straight roads like the Fosse Way across the English countryside. Soon the roads were lined with military camps for soldiers and sumptuous villas for prosperous landholders.

Feudal castles from medieval times and stately homes in all the great styles of English architecture come into view every few miles along the road. Alfred the Great's daughter established the towering castle at Warwick by the River Avon. Henry VIII was royally entertained at Compton Wynyates, and Queen Elizabeth I visited Charlecote Park. The Duke of Marlborough's noble palace of Blenheim, near Oxford, was the gift of Queen Anne after the victory of Blenheim in 1704. A century and a half

Lounging on the lawn in a Gothic setting of pinnacles and gargoyles.

later, Winston Churchill was born within its walls.

Untouched by large-scale modern industry, the villages of Shakespeare Country retain the charm of earlier times. The house in which Shakespeare himself was born will delight you with its crazy angles and well-worn floors. In the Cotswolds, every parish church has its own story. The "wool churches", for example, were financed by rich merchants who prospered in the 14th- and 15th-century heyday of the wool trade. True to the spirit of country life, church doors usually remain unlocked, even when the vicar isn't there. Stained-glass, carved stone and engraved brass memorial plaques are the pride of many a country parish.

Sightseeing is only part of the fun, however. Antique shops, craft markets and art galleries hold more than the usual treasures in store. There are horse fairs, music festivals,

THE HEART OF ENGLAND

athletic contests, sheep dog trials and folk celebrations throughout the year. You can see or participate in a wide variety of sports, especially at Oxford: rowing, rugby, soccer, cricket, tennis and squash.

Nightlife can be as sophisticated as a performance by the Royal Shakespeare Company, or as simple as a romantic tête-à-tête over a glass of sherry. Stratford's theatre season runs from March to January, and Oxford's all year long. Restaurants still serve cream teas in the afternoon, and you can always enjoy a pint of bitter in a warm, friendly pub at nightfall. For dinner, sample traditional English fare—roast beef and Yorkshire pudding, Toad-in-the-Hole or Bubble and Squeak.

The pleasures of England's heartland come into their own from May to September, though it's enjoyable to pay a visit any time of year. In spring the fields fill with wild flowers and flocks of newborn lambs. Stately homes and smaller museums generally open to visitors from April or May until September or October. The warm summer weather is ideal for cross-country hikes and bicycle tours, or you can hire a houseboat for a leisurely cruise on the region's maze of canals.

In autumn, the leaves on English oaks turn yellow, the beeches flaming red, but bright holly bushes and ropes of ivy keep the roadsides green. This is the moment to stop along the way and search the hedgerows for ripe blackberries. The days can stay fairly warm well into November.

If your visit falls in winter, there's still lots to see and do. Oxford's medieval colleges are open to visitors throughout the year, as are the Shakespearean properties in Stratford. You'll meet the English people more easily after the crowds of summer visitors have moved on. Winter is the time to appreciate the extraordinarily civilized pace of life and the low-key, natural welcome.

By definition, any visit to Oxford and Shakespeare Country turns out to be too short. Even so, it's astonishing that an afternoon in Oxford, a two-day Shakespearean pilgrimage to Stratford, or a day's dash through the Cotswold countryside can leave such vivid memories. A vision of England will stay with you for a lifetime, once you've seen its heartland.

Neat stone walls circle Snowshill; spinner demonstrates her craft.

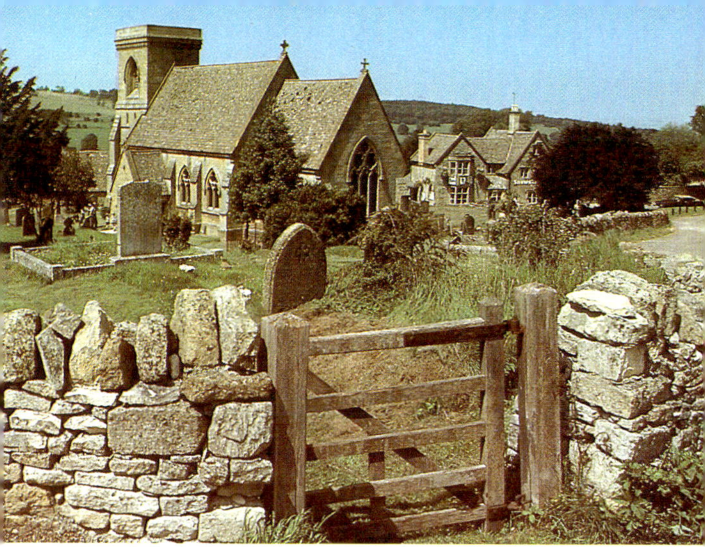

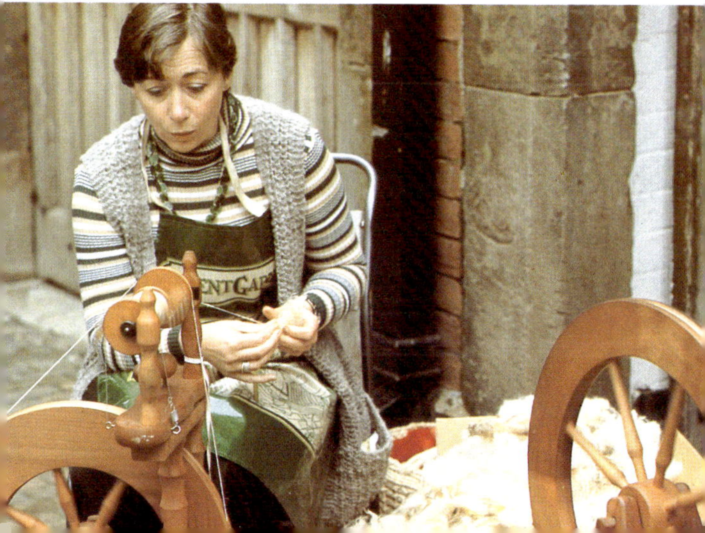

A Brief History

The "heart of England" has been at the centre of the nation's history right from the start. Neolithic man buried his dead in the "long barrows" that are scattered across the countryside, and Bronze Age inhabitants erected monolithic stone circles like the Rollright Stones in the Cotswolds. Proper history got under way in central England around 400 B.C., when the primitive population was subdued by waves of Celtic invaders. Known as Britons, they came from the Continent, bringing with them skill in forging iron tools. They ruled the land until the tread of Roman legions put them to flight.

Worthy object of study—fine Roman mosaic in Corinium Museum.

Roman Britain

Julius Caesar himself led the first Roman invasion of Britain in 55 B.C., really not much more than a scouting party. He found little of interest in the rainy island, and turned his efforts to more productive conquests in sunnier regions. But the Roman troops returned.

In the middle of the 1st century A.D., Britain became a Roman province with cities at London (Londinium) and Cirencester (Corinium) Dobunnorum), among many others. The heartland of Britain was developed with Roman roads, camps, forts and villas, and even today many traces of Roman occupation remain. But the fiercely independent Britons didn't take to their Roman overlords and many tribesmen retreated to the north and west.

Angles, Saxons and Danes

Around the year 300, the Romans received the first challenge to their rule in Britain when Saxon pirates plundered settlements along the coast. During the next two centuries, as Roman power declined and Rome itself was invaded and pillaged by northern tribes, Saxon hordes raided deep into the heart of Britain.

Unlike the Roman commanders who longed for the dry and sunny Mediterranean, the Angles and Saxons who swept across Britain came from northern Europe. The low rolling hills and lush vales of England must have seemed just like home—only better. They stayed and settled on the land, mixing with the earlier inhabitants, though the ruling class remained, at least nominally, Saxon.

In the 6th and 7th centuries, the Saxon kingdoms of Hwicce, Mercia and Wessex embraced the heart of Eng- **13** land, battling one another for power and glory. Gradually, Christianity made inroads from the Continent, and by the end of the 7th century most of the pagans had been baptized.

Raids from northern Europe were not over yet. Danish searovers plundered the English coasts and spread inland during the 9th century to establish the "Danelaw", a large region required to pay a tax (the "Danegeld") to the conquerors. Edward the Elder and his son Athelstan reconquered the Danelaw and were the first kings to rule all of England.

At this point, history becomes the stage for a cast of colourful figures whose mighty deeds (or lack of them) echo in their names. Take for instance Ethelred the Unready, a king who wasn't prepared to meet the invasion of the Danish king, Sweyn Forkbeard, in 994. Sweyn's son Canute subsequently became King of England (1016-35), ruling also over Denmark (from 1018) and Norway (1028).

But the Scandinavians lost hold when Canute died, making way for yet another invasion. In 1066 the Normans, led by William the Conqueror, stormed across the Channel and defeated the forces of Harold, England's elected king. Since the Normans' famous victory at the Battle of Hastings, no foreign power has succeeded in conquering the island kingdom.

Plantagenets and Tudors

After 1066, the Norman knights were granted huge territories and settled in—much to the indignation of the Angles and Saxons. But time went by, and the three gradually merged to form the English nation, neither totally Latin nor wholly Anglo-Saxon. The English language also evolved from the merging of Norman and Anglo-Saxon elements.

Henry II (1154–89), a Plantagenet descendant of William the Conqueror, was not only King of England, but also Duke of Normandy and Count of Anjou. As such, he ruled all of western France down to the Pyrenees. Coupling a strong Norman monarchy with the Anglo-Saxon traditions of local rule, Henry brought peace and prosperity to England. Instead of fighting feudal battles, English knights concentrated on developing the wealth of their estates. But the English possession of territory in France led in 1339 to the Hundred Years' War, a century of conflict in which England sought to consolidate its position in France. Although there were several glorious English victories (Crécy, Calais, Agincourt), the French finally won out in 1453.

Europe's greatest medieval disaster, the Black Death, invaded England in the 14th century, taking an appalling toll of lives. In 1348-49, during the reign of Edward III, almost half of England's population died. Few men were left to plough the fields and harvest

Warwick jousting tourney brings back pageantry of medieval times.

the crops. An able-bodied workman could demand whatever he wanted for his labour, and the lord of the manor would have to pay.

Unless, of course, the lord found another way to use his land. For it took dozens of men to farm several good-sized fields, but only one boy to watch over a large flock of sheep on the same land, and wool was as valuable as wheat. When Edward III coaxed some skilled Flemish weavers to settle in England and teach their craft to his subjects, the economic greatness of England was born.

The limestone bedrock and thin topsoil of the Cotswold region made the area much more profitable for sheep-grazing than for agriculture. The new industry took hold here at once, and Cotswold wool— the country's best—was sent by caravans of pack animals down to Gloucester and Bristol. There it was spun and woven, and the fine cloth was carried around the world by sea; Britain was right in the process of building up a navy.

The face of the land changed when Henry VIII dissolved the monasteries in the 1530s and turned to Protestantism. Great manor houses in Tudor style rose on former abbey lands, vast tracts of which were committed to sheep pasturage.

The Elizabethan Age

The heart of England was never more prosperous, happy or beautiful than in the age of Elizabeth I, the "Faerie Queene". The young monarch was only 25 years old when she took the throne in 1558, but she knew how to survive. Raised in an atmosphere of political intrigue and constant peril, she looked first to security—her own and that of her country. When Spain, Europe's most powerful nation, sent its Armada against her in 1588, she emerged victorious and the Spanish threat evaporated.

During Elizabeth's reign, the arts flourished. The English language acquired self-confidence in this period, taking on approximately the form it has today. In literature, the queen's reign was exceptional, producing great writers, dramatists, poets and thinkers such as Ben Jonson, John Donne, Edmund Spenser and Christopher Marlowe, overshadowed by the greatest English poet and dramatist of all— William Shakespeare. On another front, half-timbered buildings of English oak went up all over the country. In spite of

Great Elizabethans

SIR WALTER RALEIGH (c. 1552–1618). Soldier and courtier knighted in 1584. In the vanguard of the early settlement of America, Raleigh founded colonies in Virginia and off the coast of North Carolina. He travelled to South America, bringing back to England tales of rich gold mines—and the potato. After 13 years' imprisonment in the Tower of London for conspiring against James I, he again took up the search for South American gold. He returned to England empty-handed and was beheaded for his failure.

EDMUND SPENSER (c. 1552–99). Poet and author of the ambitious six-book epic poem, *The Faerie Queene*, dedicated to Queen Elizabeth. Written in Spenserian verse, a special form devised by the poet, the work is full of patriotic allegories in praise of the queen and her virtues.

NICHOLAS HILLIARD (c. 1547–1619). Artist famed for his jewel-like miniature portraits of Queen Elizabeth and the Tudor aristocracy. His miniatures were intended to be held in the hand and admired at close range.

JOHN DONNE (1572–1631). One of the "metaphysical poets", an Anglican priest and Dean of St. Paul's. Renowned both for the sensual poems of his early years and his later religious poems and sermons.

CHRISTOPHER MARLOWE (1564–93). One of the greatest dramatists and poets of his time. The author of such tragedies as *Tamburlaine*, *The Jew of Malta* and *Doctor Faustus*, his masterpiece. Marlowe was transcended by William Shakespeare, whom, ironically, he influenced strongly.

SIR FRANCIS DRAKE (c. 1540–96). Privateer, admiral and explorer. After carrying out many successful raids on Spanish settlements in the Caribbean, Drake was commissioned by Queen Elizabeth to undertake a voyage of discovery in 1577. He circumnavigated the globe in three years and was knighted for the exploit. Drake helped defeat the Spanish Armada in 1588, one of the greatest English naval victories and a turning point in the nation's history.

BEN JONSON (c. 1573–1637). Dramatist and poet, ranked alongside Marlowe and Shakespeare. From employment as a bricklayer, soldier and actor, Ben Jonson turned to writing plays. He is best remembered for three brilliant comedies, *The Alchemist, Every Man in His Humour* and *Volpone, or The Fox*.

their flimsy appearance, the buildings were as sturdy as the oak itself, and many survive today in Stratford, Warwick and villages all over the area.

Civil War

A generation after Shakespeare's death, England was torn by civil war. Elizabeth died without an heir, and James I was rapidly brought down from Scotland. Although the country was staunchly Protestant, the Catholics represented a powerful force, within and without. Charles I, who succeeded to the throne in 1625, alienated all the important factions in his kingdom, one by one. In 1642, fighting broke out between the Royalists ("Cavaliers")—supported by the nobles, the Church of England and the Catholics—and the Puritan parliamentary forces ("Roundheads")—entrenched in London and backed by the tradesmen. The country lost its monarch and the monarch lost his head.

Following the execution of Charles in 1649, England became a commonwealth and then a protectorate (1653) under the dreary Puritan rule of Oliver Cromwell, the Lord Protector. But in 1660, two years after Cromwell's death, a monarch was back on the throne of England, and cheerful crowds hailed the beginning of Charles II's reign.

England's political troubles weren't over, however. James II, who followed Charles, converted to Roman Catholicism, an impossible situation in the largely Protestant country. The

bloodless "Glorious Revolution" overthrew him in 1688, and he fled the country to be replaced by William and Mary of the Protestant House of Orange.

World of Shakespeare shows how people lived in the Tudor era.

Britannia Rules

Though the political scene may have been in turmoil, England's power on the seas and in distant lands continued to grow. What had once been a hardship post for low-ranking Roman governors was now the centre of an ever-expanding empire. England was a

prime player in the European game of power politics.

In 1701, Louis XIV of France attempted to tip the balance of power in his favour by placing his grandson on the throne of Spain. England considered this grounds for war, and English armies led by the Duke of Marlborough went on to triumph in the War of the Spanish Succession. To express the gratitude of the nation, Queen Anne gave her victorious general a vast estate just outside Oxford. The house she set out to build for him— Blenheim Palace—was worthy of a great monarch and an ascendant nation.

Throughout the 18th century, Englishmen lived in a manner befitting the people of a prosperous and powerful nation. New and splendid buildings rose throughout the land, and the export of wool continued to bring enormous wealth. In Stratford-upon-Avon, a new Town Hall in the Georgian style went up in 1767, two years after the 200th anniversary of Shakespeare's birth. The townspeople decided to celebrate Shakespeare's Jubilee in the new hall, belatedly or not, and in 1769 elaborate festivities were arranged. David Garrick, the foremost Shakespearean actor of the day, presented a bust of the Bard which now stands high on the Town Hall wall. There were dances, horse races, speeches and concerts, but astonishingly little of Shakespeare's work was read or performed.

The 1770s brought a challenge to the supremacy of English government when colonists in America rose in revolt. Though nominally English, many Americans had been born in the New World and looked upon it as their native country. George Washington grew up in Virginia and never visited the house in Sulgrave, near Banbury, that his great-grandfather had left to seek his fortune in the colonies (see p. 45).

After the English defeat in America, the European struggle with Napoleon began. England was to be victorious against the French, but even greater turmoil was brewing within England's heartland.

The Industrial Revolution

If England had been rich before the coming of the modern age, the country was to grow immensely richer once the machines of industry were powered by steam. Mines, factories and transport hummed, and enterprising businessmen made fortunes in no time. But England's working people were anything but rich. Lured from poor villages into the cities, they were rewarded with bad living conditions and low wages. Meanwhile, the countryside, deprived of their labour, became even poorer.

The supremacy of wool was challenged by cheap cotton, and the hand loom in a cosy Cotswold house by gargantuan steam-driven factory machines. Oxford and some other cities took their share of the new wealth by welcoming industry, but many once-proud towns became half-deserted skeletons of their medieval selves. The men who lived in the great country houses built in Tudor times preserved their power and influence, but industrialization was to change their lives as well.

From Victorian England to Modern Times

Queen Victoria's reign (1837–1901)—the age of steam and iron, of transport, communications and commerce—saw the emergence of Great Britain as an imperial power. But in the heart of England, the exodus from the countryside accelerated. During the agricultural depression of the 1880s, many villagers left their homeland for a better life in Canada, Australia or South Africa.

After two world wars and the spread of business and urbanization, the land's fortunes changed once again. Tired of the pressures of city life, people began to move back to the beautiful villages passed over by the grimy hand of industry. First were artists and craftsmen, who came in search of picturesque scenes and cheap rent, then retired people fleeing noise and pollution. When the war damage was swept away and production returned to normal, automobiles provided the freedom to live in the country and work in the city. Cars brought tourists, too, and tourists brought prosperity.

Stratford has always had its other pursuits—as a cattle market and local transport hub—and tourists have been coming to visit Shakespeare's birthplace for centuries. Oxford's importance has never waned, as over the years the university educated many of the men who would lead the nation in the realms of statecraft, business and the arts. But modern times have proved a boon to the entire region, bringing wealth to preserve the precious legacy of past ages. **21**

Where to Go

Setting out for Shakespeare Country from London, the natural itinerary takes you first to Oxford, 1½ hours away by train, bus or car. You'll want to linger there awhile before you head north for Stratford (39 miles away), a good base for touring Shakespeare Country. Go out from here to scout

Inspired by the gentle Cotswold landscape, amateur artists set brush to paper in Upper Slaughter. Stained glass embellishes Northleach church.

round villages and towns in the Cotswold Hills; and when the time comes to return to London, you can travel by bus or train from the Cotswold town of Moreton-in-Marsh. In this way, you take in the academic atmosphere of a great centre of learning, get to know the birthplace and surround-ings of England's greatest playwright and explore the most charming and typical region in the heartland of England.

For detailed information about travelling to the area from London, plus advice on inter-city coaches and trains, see TRANSPORT, pages 124–6.

Oxford

If you're visiting Oxford for just a few hours, you won't want to—nor can you—look at each of the 34 colleges. Concentrate instead on the great ones and try to catch the feel of student life and traditions. You'll carry away an impression of magnificent cream stone buildings; beautiful parks, lawns and gardens; an ambience of hallowed antiquity and hushed scholarship.

As you tour Oxford, it's important to remember that the colleges and other buildings of interest all have different visiting hours. Generally, the colleges are open at least from 2–4 p.m., though many have longer hours in the evening and some can be visited in the morning. Be sure to ask at the Oxford Information Centre in St. Aldate's Street for brochures and a list of hours.

When a college is open, the chances are good that its chapel will be, too. Try the door, and don't hesitate to walk in.

As you stroll through town, refer to the map opposite. Few colleges bear signs giving their names, and without a map, you won't know whether you're gazing at Merton or Magdalen.

From Easter to the end of October, walking tours of Oxford and its colleges are organized by the Information Centre. Tours leave from the Centre several times a day, Monday to Saturday, and last for about two hours. A small charge is made, but it's a sensible way of getting the most out of a visit.

City Sights

Start your walking tour of Oxford at **Carfax,** the intersection of Queen Street, Cornmarket, the High and St. Aldate's; this is the hub of the town. The crossing is dominated by the 14th-century **Carfax Tower,** once part of St. Martin's Church and still used as a look-out point. Climb to the top for a magnificent view over Oxford's skyline of Gothic pinnacles and spires. Every 15 minutes the "quarter boys" in the tower take a whack at the bells to chime the quarter-hour.

A few yards down the gentle hill from Carfax on St. Aldate's, you'll see Oxford's Town Hall and the City Museum, with displays outlining local history. Continue down and you soon come to one of the university's outstanding landmarks. **Tom Tower,**

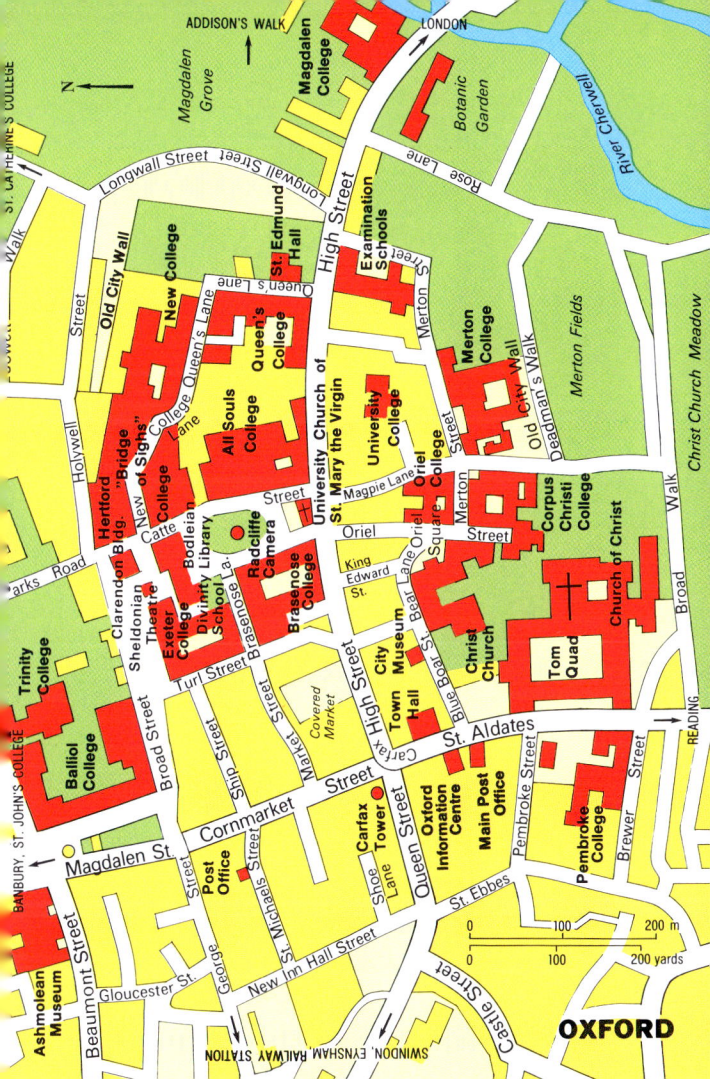

OXFORD

*Tom Tower of Christ Church—
an Oxford University landmark.*

which crowns the entrance to
Christ Church. The tower,
dedicated to St. Thomas of
Canterbury, was begun shortly after Cardinal Wolsey
founded the college in 1525.
Most visitors don't notice
that the "Gothic" style of
the upper part—completed in
1682 by Christopher Wren—
differs considerably from the
Tudor base erected in Wolsey's time. Great Tom, the bell
in the tower, still chimes 101
times at 9.05 each evening
(the time when the original 101
students were called in).

Pass through Memorial
Gate and visit the three inter-
connecting "quads", or quadrangles, that make this one of
the biggest colleges; the middle quad, Peck, is traditionally
the haunt of Britain's aristocracy. Lewis Carroll, Dean of
Christ Church, lodged in Canterbury Quad. He looked out
from his room over the garden—and *Alice in Wonderland*
suddenly came to life.

Climb up the flight of stairs
to the impressive 16th-century
dining hall, hung with portraits of the great and famous
who once "ate their commons"

here as humble undergraduates. Notice, too, the splendid hammerbeam ceiling*.

The **Church of Christ,** right within the college buildings, gave Christ Church its name. It's been Oxford's Anglican cathedral church since the time of Henry VIII. Parts of the structure date back even further, to the 12th century, when the Priory of St. Frideswide stood on this site. The fan vaulting in the chancel will impress you, as will the tracery windows that decorate Lady and Latin chapels. You may also want to have a look at **Christ Church Picture Gallery,** a permanent collection of outstanding Old Master paintings and drawings. Signs inside the college point the way to the entrance.

Pembroke College, founded in 1624, lies across the street from Christ Church. Make your way to Chapel Quad, formed by a harmonious array of buildings that date from the founding to the present. The richly ornamented 18th-century chapel has a beautiful ceiling painted in the style of Raphael, although much of the decoration was added in Victorian times. The "Gothic"

---

* For a description of architectural terms and styles, see box, pp. 42–3.

stained-glass, for example, was added in 1884.

Now go back up to Carfax and turn to your right into "the High", as it's known in Oxford parlance, a long, curving street full of surprises and good shopping. At the top end, down a passageway, lurks the town's old covered market—a fascinating jumble of craft shops and butchers, bakers and fishmongers.

"The High" is not all shopping though; it's lined with some of Oxford's finest college buildings as well. **Brasenose College** (enter from Radcliffe Square) probably takes its name from a bronze door knocker or handle in the shape of a nose which is now enshrined in the dining hall. It is thought to have been in service on the gate of a 13th-century hall which stood here. All the buildings surrounding Old Quad date from the 16th century, and the chapel is notable for its vaulted ceiling, a superb example of the Gothic Revival style.

Oriel College in Oriel Square (properly known as the "House of the Blessed Virgin Mary in Oxford") was named after a house called La Oriole, acquired by the college shortly after its founding in 1326. Have a look at the entrance to **27**

Town and Gown

Long before Oxford had a university, it was a market town conveniently situated at the junction of the rivers Cherwell (pronounced Charwell) and Thames. Only after 1167 did it begin to develop into what was to become the most famous university town in the English-speaking world. That was the year King Henry II forbade English scholars to study at the Sorbonne. They decided to set up at Oxford instead.

Even before Oxford had colleges, it had competition. Cambridge University was founded in 1209 by a group of Oxford scholars who made their way east. They had fled the wrath of townsfolk, upset by the youthful exuberance and wild behaviour of many university students (the "gown"). Over the centuries, Oxford and Cambridge developed side by side, their comparable achievements making rivalry inevitable.

The first colleges were residence halls where students could be kept under some sort of control and discouraged from drinking and brawling. Students were members of minor religious orders. They followed long courses of logic and Latin grammar (the "Trivium" and "Quadrivium"), attending lectures in black academic gowns. The student "problem" in Oxford isn't new, and there were many fights between "town and gown".

Gradually, the colleges attracted endowments and grew richer than the university, or corporate body, which controlled final examinations. Colleges coached students for the exams and were governed by a head (called the Provost, Master, Warden or Dean) and Fellows, members with teaching or research appointments, often elected for life. They had to remain celibate until Victorian times. Nowadays, the development of medical and scientific research facilities has brought money back to the university, for only through government grants can modern educational needs be met.

Today, few undergraduates learn Latin or take religious orders. They live in college one, or at most two, years and the wearing of academic gowns is no longer compulsory in town. But traditions die hard at Oxford and vestiges of the strict discipline of earlier centuries are felt. New colleges are still being founded to accommodate the university's 12,000 students and its "dons" (from the Latin *dominus*, "master" or "teacher"), gathered in academic

garb, above. Women's colleges have flourished this century, and all of the university's most ancient men's colleges have opened their heavy oak doors to women.

Although the university provides overall administration, colleges are very independent in many respects and choose their own students. Through the ages, they have acquired certain reputations: Balliol for intellectual brilliance, Christ Church for its aristocratic tone, Merton for poets, Jesus College for Welshmen, Oriel for would-be vicars, St. Edmund Hall for the sporting, and so on.

The Radcliffe Camera looms large on the Oxford skyline, an imposing sight of cream-coloured stone, lofty cupolas and medieval spires.

the dining hall. The Virgin Mary stands in majesty at the top of the porch, with kings Edward II (Oriel's founder) and Charles I beneath.

The college is identified with the Oxford Movement, which called for the reform of the Church of England early in the 19th century. Several of the group's leaders, includ-ing John Keble and Cardinal Newman, were educated here.

The **University Church of St. Mary the Virgin** stands across the High from Oriel. During its long and eventful histo-ry, St. Mary's has been used as a library, lecture room, court room and auditorium. The church is an impressive example of the Perpendicular

style, a form of Gothic architecture popular in England from about 1350 to 1550. Restored last century, it's now a favourite with tourists who for a small fee can admire the spectacular view from the bell tower of Oxford's spires.

As you go down the High, you'll see quaint old buildings housing shops and banks. Now turn off for a moment into Catte Street, which runs alongside St. Mary's, for a look at the exterior of the **Radcliffe**

Camera ("chamber"). Built in the mid-1700s as a library, the circular structure with its elegant dome stands alone in a patch of greenery. It was designed during the heyday of Palladianism, the English revival of the Italian architect Andrea Palladio's classical style. The Radcliffe Camera now serves as an offshoot reading room of the Bodleian, Oxford's university library (see pp. 36–7).

All Souls College, just across Catte Street from the Radcliffe Camera, was founded in 1438. This is the only college that restricts its membership to Fellows, members of the university who have teaching or research appointments.

The "souls" in All Souls belong to the soldiers who died in the Hundred Years' War between England and France (see p. 15). King Henry VI and Archbishop Chichele, who founded the college, ordered that memorial prayers be said in the chapel for the glorious dead.

The beautiful **chapel,** the glitter of its gilded screen and the glow of the medieval stained-glass on a sunny day are unforgettable. The 15th-century hammerbeam ceiling is decorated with angels and the finely carved reredos (the

31

screen behind the altar) dates from the same period, but the figures on the reredos were destroyed by zealous reformers in Cromwellian times and replaced only in 1872.

Leave Catte Street and continue down the High to **University College.** Although founded in 1280, the college has no buildings constructed before 1634. But everything was done in a suitably Gothic style, as you'll see in the 18th-century gateway to Radcliffe Quad, with its massive carved doors and fan-vaulting. Be sure to visit the chapel, distinguished by Abraham van Linge's fine stained-glass windows of 1641. Look, too, for the memorial to the poet Shelley, who was expelled from University College when he refused to admit he had written an atheist pamphlet.

Next comes **Queen's College** (1341), named after Queen Philippa, the wife of Edward III. The statue of another queen, George II's wife, Caroline, graces the cupola above the entrance to Front Quad. Most of the existing college buildings date from the 17th and 18th centuries. Several are attributed to Christopher Wren, including the handsome library completed in 1695 and the chapel, decorated with van Linge glass and a baroque painting of the *Ascension* by James Thornhill.

Farther along the High stands the grandiose **Examination Schools** building, a 19th-century pot-pourri of historical styles. For most of the year, these lofty chambers resound to the drone of lecturers and the scribbling of undergraduates, but the university pulse speeds up in June during final examinations, or "schools", after which spontaneous champagne parties with exulting students in gowns and mortarboards are likely to be seen celebrating the end of exam agony.

Two distinguished colleges are hidden off the High in Merton Street. **Merton College,** dating from 1264, claims to be Oxford's oldest. The 14th-century Mob Quad was the very first college quadrangle. The library, again one of England's oldest, is well worth a look, and the plan of the chapel, begun around 1290 and designed without a nave, set a precedent for many others in Oxford. Later addi-

It's over! Champagne corks pop outside Examination Schools as post-exam revels get underway.

tions include the pinnacled 15th-century tower.

Corpus Christi College (1517), next door to Merton, boasts a curious sundial made in 1581; it stands in the handsome Front Quad. On top of the sundial perches a pelican, the college mascot for over three and a half centuries. The perpetual calendar is a later addition. The library contains a worthy collection of old books, protected by an 18th-century system of chains and locks. In the chapel is an altarpiece attributed to the great Flemish painter, Peter Paul Rubens.

If you're still in the mood, retrace your steps to the High and continue on down it until one of Oxford's most spacious and harmonious colleges comes into view. **Magdalen** (pronounced "maudlin"), founded in 1458 by William of Waynflete, Bishop of Winchester, delights the eye with its extensive lawns, gardens

and deer park, its beautiful Gothic cloister and Perpendicular bell tower. On the first day of May, college choristers gather at 6 a.m. to sing a Latin hymn of praise from the tower.

Worthy of note are the magnificent carved oak screen in the dining hall and the abundant ornamentation in the **chapel,** a hallmark of the Decorated Gothic style. The River

Quadrangle at Magdalen College follows typical Oxford arrangement: chapel, dining hall, lodgings and common rooms are all grouped together.

Cherwell flows past the college, and Addison's Walk—named after the 18th-century poet, journalist (some say the first true one) and member of the college—winds through its "water meadows".

From the northern reaches of Addison's Walk, you catch a glimpse of one of the colleges founded this century—**St. Catherine's** (1963). The entire complex, furniture and all, was designed by the Danish architect Arne Jacobsen. Its geometrical conception harmonizes remarkably well with Oxford architecture.

Across the High from Magdalen is the triumphal arch of Danby Gateway, which leads to the university's 17th-century **Botanic Garden,** an artfully designed "laboratory" of medicinal plants and herbs, extensive greenhouses and rock and rose gardens. Beyond, the green swath of Merton Fields and Christ Church Meadow stretches down to the college boat house beside the River Cherwell. Here's where the Oxford team trains for its annual race against Cambridge.

This is as far as it's worth going in this direction, so head back towards Carfax along the High and turn into Queen's Lane to track down more Oxford landmarks. At the crossroad stands **St. Edmund Hall,** affectionately known as Teddy Hall. St. Edmund, built in 1270, is the only hall to have survived in its original shape, though artfully concealed modern additions keep the college's facilities in line with the times. The first Oxford colleges were modest **35**

medieval halls (or hostels) like this. The small chapel contains stained-glass decorated in the Pre-Raphaelite style by William Morris and Edward Burne-Jones.

Queen's Lane runs into New College Lane, where you'll find the entrance to **New College,** one of the university's most venerable complexes. William of Wykeham, Bishop of Winchester, founded the college in 1379 and he is largely responsible for its plan.

The chapel, one of Oxford's largest and finest, contains a breathtaking reredos installed in the 19th century. Sir Joshua Reynolds designed the glass in the West Window portraying the *Nativity* and *Seven Virtues.* The painting of *St. James* is the work of El Greco. Near it, in a glass safe, you can see the glittering pastoral staff that belonged to William of Wykeham, known to members of the college as "the Founder". His statue and some mementoes remind New College undergraduates to this day of the bishop's beneficence. The tortured statue of *Lazarus* in the chapel entrance was sculpted by Sir Jacob Epstein in 1951.

Before you leave the college, stroll in the beautiful gardens, which contain a section of Oxford's medieval city wall.

Constructed in the reign of Henry II, the wall was fortified with bastions and a walkway for sentries.

New College Lane has its own "Bridge of Sighs"—a modern copy of the one in Venice—but here the bridge merely joins two buildings belonging to Hertford College.

Pass under the bridge and make your way to Broad Street, the heart of academic Oxford. Here stands the graceful **Sheldonian Theatre,** guarded by a phalanx of dour busts of Roman emperors (modern copies of the 19th-century originals). This was the first building designed by Christopher Wren, a young professor of astronomy who went on to become one of England's greatest architects.

Commissioned by Gilbert Sheldon, Archbishop of Canterbury, in 1633, the theatre is used for academic ceremonies and concerts. On one celebrated occasion, Josef Haydn received an honorary Doctor of Music degree, followed by a performance of his "Oxford Symphony". Visitors are welcome to admire the splendid view of Oxford from the Sheldonian's cupola.

Not far away stands Oxford's world-famous library, the **Bodleian.** A magnificent old

room holds the collection of Humphrey, Duke of Gloucester, which forms the nucleus of the Bodleian's present reserve of three million volumes. The duke donated his library to the Bodleian in 1425, but it was broken up during the Reformation. Thanks to the initiative of Sir Thomas Bodley, a graduate of Magdalen, a new library was established in 1602. According to an arrangement he made with the Stationers' Company, the Bod-

The ornate vaulted ceiling and priceless rare books vie for attention in the Divinity School.

leian is entitled to a copy of every book printed in England.

Rare books, including a Shakespeare First Folio, are on view in the adjoining building, known as the **Divinity School.** Once a lecture hall, the Divinity School is noted for the beauty of its 15th-cen- **37** tury Perpendicular Gothic architecture and elaborate stone vault.

Nearby **Exeter College** (1314) has a neo-Gothic chapel. It was designed by the eminent Victorian architect Sir Gilbert Scott, who took his inspiration from the Sainte-Chapelle in Paris. The rich interior, with its stained-glass, marble and mosaics, provides the perfect setting for Edward Burne-Jones' tapestry of the *Adoration of the Magi*. Take a look, too, at the Gothic Revival dining hall, a 17th-century version of medieval décor.

Balliol College is entered from Broad Street. Balliol is another of the university's medieval colleges (founded in 1263), but its buildings date mostly from the 19th century. In the dining hall of 1877 are portraits of great Balliol men, a daunting array of worthies who went out to rule the world.

Now make your way to Magdalen Street, past the **Martyrs' Memorial** to the Protestant bishops—Cranmer, Latimer and Ridley—who were burned at the stake by "Bloody Mary". Then turn into fashionable Beaumont Street for a look at the **Ashmolean Museum.** The Greek-style building was designed in 1841 to house the art and archaeological treasures donated to the university over the centuries. The excellent display of Italian works include superb Michelangelo and Raphael drawings. Important paintings by the Pre-Raphaelites hang in their own gallery, just one of the museum's 73 rooms. Also on view is a fine selection of ceramic pieces: Worcester porcelain, English Delftware and Italian majolica.

The Anglo-Saxon antiquities include the **Alfred Jewel,** a rare portrait in enamel of the good King Alfred. Some of the spectacular finds from Sir Arthur Evans' excavations at Knossos in Crete and Sir Flinders Petrie's digs in Egypt have also made their way to the Ashmolean. Entry to the museum is free, so plan several visits if you can.

Another historic college, **St. John's,** stands just across St. Giles Street. The college was founded by Archbishop Chichele in 1437 as a Cistercian institution, and some of the buildings that form Front Quad were occupied by Cistercian scholars. Go through the fan-vaulted passage to Canterbury Quad. The impressive baroque ranges are decorated with statues of King Charles I and Queen Henrietta Maria.

Living in College

Despite the addition of some amenities, most Oxford colleges are as austere as the medieval monastic complexes that inspired their plan. College buildings—including a chapel and dining hall (like that of Christ Church, right), common rooms and lodgings —are grouped around "quads" (quadrangles) and surrounded by gardens, meadows or parkland.

Undergraduates live in simple bedrooms and sitting rooms that tend to be very cold. To ensure a maximum of privacy, the rooms are situated around staircases, rather than along corridors. Most rooms have heavy oak doors in addition to ordinary ones. When both doors are closed, a student is said to be "sporting his oak", *i.e.* he doesn't want to be disturbed.

Servants are assigned to all the undergraduates who live in college (one for about 10 to 15). Known as "scouts", they wake the students in their charge each morning and check on their presence. Servants ease the burdens of academic life by making the beds, doing the cleaning and organizing dinner parties. Each student cultivates the friendship of his scout—and buys him frequent beers for services rendered.

Oxford Environs

The Oxford area is peppered with country houses and manors that can be visited by the public. Many contain major treasures, some are interesting as buildings, others for their associations, special attractions (gardens, aviaries, animal parks and miniature trains) or for the activities held in their grounds (sheep dog trials, jousting, etc.). The selection that follows is an arbitrary one. There are so many interesting houses within reach of Oxford that it's impossible to see even a fraction of them on a short visit.

Blenheim Palace. The Duke of Marlborough's splendid palace, one of England's most impressive sights, lies just 8 miles north-west of Oxford. You can join a conducted tour to visit Blenheim, or take a bus from Oxford to WOODSTOCK, the village to which the palace belongs.

A residence sumptuous enough for royalty, Blenheim symbolizes English greatness in the time of Queen Anne. The Queen undertook to build the palace for John Churchill, first Duke of Marlborough, after he led the English to victory in the crucial battle at Blenheim (see p. 20).

The duke never saw the palace in its finished state, though he chose Sir John Vanbrugh as architect and approved the imposing baroque design. Hundreds of thousands of pounds were spent and more than two decades elapsed before the great residence was completed.

Guides will show you around Blenheim, pointing out its priceless furnishings and recounting its romantic history. The palace is enormous, filled

Blenheim, residence of a duke and an English baroque masterpiece, doesn't at all impress the cows.

40

with treasures and surrounded by enchanting formal gardens. It's now inhabited by the 11th Duke of Marlborough and his wife. If the ducal flag is flying, His Grace is in residence.

In the **Great Hall,** you'll see a picture of John Churchill presenting a plan of the Battle of Blenheim to Britannia. The duke's exploits are further glorified on the ceiling of the saloon, painted by the Frenchman Louis Laguerre, and in the tapestries of Judocus de Vos in the **state rooms.**

The palace is embellished throughout with ornamental stucco work, carved marble and gilding. The purple marble fireplaces in the state rooms are the work of Grinling Gibbons, and the elaborate marble doorway in the **Long Library** is by Nicholas Hawksmoor, Vanbrugh's assistant. The chapel contains the tomb of John Churchill, his wife and two sons, all of whom are shown in Classical attire.

John Churchill's illustrious descendant, Winston Churchill, was born in a room on the ground floor on November 30, 1874. The parents of England's great war-time leader were Lord Randolph Churchill, brother of the eighth duke, and Jennie Jerome, an American.

The ABCs of English Architecture

Some of England's most important architectural monuments lie in the heartland of the country. To help you appreciate these magnificent buildings to the full, we've summarized here the significant styles you'll come across and vocabulary you'll hear as you tour the area.

Norman (1066–1190). This local form of the Romanesque was brought over by William the Conqueror and his Norman knights. Typical features include thick walls, small windows and massive masonry, low towers, rounded arches and elaborately carved mouldings.

Gothic (1190–1550). The pointed arch, the hallmark of Gothic construction, was introduced into England in the 12th century by Cistercian monks. Over the next 400 years, English builders evolved three distinct variations of the style: Early English (1190–1300), Decorated (1280–1350) and Perpendicular (1330–1550).

The distinguishing feature of **Early English** buildings is their long, narrow windows. Two or three, perhaps as many as seven, windows were grouped together to admit a maximum of light.

In the **Decorated** period, windows grew considerably wider, and they were ornamented with tracery (patterns in stone). The S-curve motif appeared everywhere—in tracery, on arches and around doorways.

True to its name, **Perpendicular** architecture reverted to unadorned horizontals and verticals. Tracery lost its fantasy and the arched "panel motif" predominates. Typical of the period are hammerbeam roofs (of carved wood with projecting supports and exposed beams) and fan vaulting, an intricate array of ribs and panels.

Tudor (†520–1600). Tudor buildings generally continued the Gothic spirit, despite a veneer of Italian Renaissance decoration. King Henry VIII gave the new Italian style his official patronage, but it took hold in the country very slowly. Stately homes were often of brick, with characteristic "twisted" chimneys. Ordinary houses were still built in half-timbered style, a framework of wood filled in with plaster.

During the reign of Queen Elizabeth I, new structural principles such as the symmetry of façades were adopted. But the so-called **Elizabethan** (1560–1600) style was just as much Gothic as it was Renaissance.

Late Renaissance (1625–1700). Sir Christopher Wren single-handedly popularized the Renaissance style in England, beginning with his design for Oxford's Sheldonian Theatre. Classical domes and columns and rectangular windows came into general use, with symmetry and harmony as the guiding principles.

Baroque (1700–50). Monumental scale, dramatic curving forms and sweeping vistas are the characteristics of baroque buildings. Although Wren's later work displays some baroque features, the chief practitioners of the style were John Vanbrugh, architect of Blenheim, and his assistant, Nicholas Hawksmoor.

Palladianism (1720–50). Lord Burlington and his disciple, William Kent, championed the approach to architecture of Italy's Andrea Palladio (1500–80). Prominent in their work are Roman temple fronts and classical details, comparable both in design and handling to the antique originals.

Picturesque. In the 18th century, landscape gardeners transformed the English countryside into an ideal suggested by the paintings of the French artists Claude Lorrain and Gaspard Poussin. To achieve the necessary ruggedness and asymmetry, river courses were altered, forests of trees artfully planted and monumental lakes created.

Greek Revival (1780–1840). When James "Athenian" Stuart designed England's first Greek-style building in 1758, he had few imitators. But the severe and simple style began to catch on some 20 years later, and by the 1820s buildings all over the country sported Doric porticos and Ionic columns.

Regency (1810–37). During the Regency of the Prince of Wales, architecture ranged from the austere simplicity of Sir John Soane's designs to the sumptuous exoticism of John Nash. But use of classical orders or proportions was common to all. Elegant terraced houses and gay villas of gleaming white stucco went up in spa towns like Cheltenham. The buildings were adorned with cast-iron window canopies, verandahs, balconies and railings embellished with eclectic motifs: Greek lyres, Gothic arches or Chinese pagodas.

Victorian Style (1837–90). Romantics at heart, 19th-century architects looked to the past for suitable building styles. They tried their hand at everything from Perpendicular Gothic (favoured for churches) to Grecian. Some designs adhered closely to historical models, while others interpreted or adapted venerable styles. Even when façades and decoration appear fairly authentic, the sophisticated floor plans of the "revivals" separate them from their illustrious architectural forebears. **43**

After the tour, stroll through the formal **gardens and park.** The sweeping vistas across manicured grounds are magnificent. You'll see a towering victory column, monumental bridge and serenely beautiful lake, created by the 18th-century landscape gardener "Capability" Brown. Refreshments are served in the restaurant, installed in what was once the palace dairy.

Before you leave the Blenheim area, visit the charming village of Woodstock and Sir Winston's tomb in the churchyard at nearby Bladon.

Waddesdon Manor (29 miles north-east of Oxford near AYLESBURY). Baron Ferdinand de Rothschild's grand French Renaissance-style chateau was built in 1889 as a showcase for his magnificent collection of French 18th-century decorative art. On view are exquisite examples of Meissen and Sèvres porcelain and the best of the cabinetmaker's art. There's also a wealth of paintings by Boucher, Watteau, Gainsborough, Reynolds and Romney. Apart from mementoes of the Rothschild family,

Just one key opens this intricate lock at Blenheim—an ingenious mechanism and superb work of art.

the exhibits of costumes, lace, buttons and textiles are also of great interest.

Sulgrave Manor. Some 30 miles north of Oxford lies the hamlet of SULGRAVE, a shrine for American visitors. This pretty village was the ancestral home of George Washington. Lawrence Washington purchased the land from Henry VIII in 1539, and the house he built, with its mullioned windows and beamed ceilings, is both comfortable and attractive. The fine period furnishings on display were gathered together when the house was restored. Choice pieces in the collection include a Gilbert Stuart portrait of George Washington. The house, gardens and little village are so pleasant that it is surprising Colonel John Washington (George's great-grandfather) left here in 1656 to be mate on a small English ship bound for America.

Compton Wynyates. The serenity of this picturesque Tudor mansion (33 miles north-west of Oxford), Lord Northampton's Warwickshire residence, contrasts with the busy town life of nearby BANBURY (immortalized in the famous 18th-century nursery rhyme). "Twisted" chimneys and crenellated walls of pink brick, **45**

Banbury Cross

All English-speaking children can recite the historic nursery rhyme about Banbury, first published in 1784:

Ride a cock-horse to Banbury Cross,
To see a fine lady upon a white horse.
Rings on her fingers and bells on her toes,
And she shall have music wherever she goes.

In medieval times, certain towns displaying crosses could hold weekly markets— a special privilege granted by royal charter. Banbury was one those towns.

No one knows for sure what happened to Banbury Cross. It may have been destroyed by Puritan zealots in the civil war. In 1859, a new "Gothic" cross commemorating the marriage of England's Princess Royal to the Crown Prince of Prussia was put up in the centre of town. Statues of Queen Victoria and Kings Edward VII and George V were added later.

Whatever the history, the town's fame spread far and wide. Today, it's hard to see why so much fuss was made about such an ordinary little town. Sad to say, even Banbury cakes with crosses on them, a speciality of the Lenten season, are better sampled elsewhere.

mullioned windows and half-timbering charm the eye. The porch bears the arms of Henry VIII, who visited the house not long after its completion in 1520.

Ancestral portraits and the original furniture fill the cosy rooms of Compton Wynyates. You'll see a tapestry designed by the 16th-century Italian master Giulio Romano and one of the rare paintings by the Venetian artist, Giorgione. But many visitors come just to stroll through the renowned topiary garden (with trees and shrubs trimmed in ornamental shapes) and to enjoy the verdant countryside.

More Stately Homes

There are so many historic houses in the Oxford area that it's impossible to see them all. If you have the time, you may want to visit **Kingston House** in KINGSTON BAGPUIZE (9 miles south-west of Oxford), a 17th-century manor house surrounded by lovely gardens. You have to make an appointment in advance to view the Norman defences and Elizabethan features of **Hinton Manor,** not far away in HINTON WALDRIST. And a most attractive topiary garden awaits you at **Buscot Park** (22 miles south-west of Oxford). This elegant 18th-century residence has fine period furnishings, Old Master paintings and a group of pictures by Edward Burne-Jones.

Of considerable architectural significance is **Rousham Park** (12 miles north of Oxford), since it was remodelled in opulent Italianate style by the eminent designer William Kent. His naturalistic design for Rousham's park created a new style in landscape gardening known as the Picturesque.

A wide moat surrounds **Broughton Castle** (20 miles north-west of Oxford), a beautifully preserved Tudor mansion that dates from 1300. There are exquisite plaster ceilings throughout and good period furniture. Broughton owes its cosy air to the fact that it's still a family house.

Huntsmen in scarlet jackets ride to hounds: the sport is favoured by England's country gentry.

Stratford-upon-Avon

Since its incorporation as a town in 1553, Stratford-upon-Avon has seen innumerable country markets and fairs and almost ceaseless horse-trading. But most of this activity goes unnoticed by visitors, who come to Stratford for only one reason: to pay tribute to William Shakespeare. Five of the buildings most closely associated with Shakespeare's life and family are under the protection of the Shakespeare Birthplace Trust. You'll save money when you visit them by buying a combination ticket to all five.

Shakespeare's Birthplace in Henley Street looks very much as it did at the time of his birth to John and Mary Arden Shakespeare. Nothing more substantial than long tradition maintains that William was born in the bedroom on the upper floor. But literary pilgrims have come to pay homage here for centuries. Many of them left their names or initials scratched in the glass of the ancient windows; nowadays a Guest Register is kept near the entrance to record visits.

Although the house remained in the possession of Shakespeare's descendants for three centuries after the poet's death, no thought was given to its preservation. It served as an inn, The Swan and Maidenhead, and suffered drastic structural changes. But modern restoration has worked miracles, as a pictorial exhibit shows.

Near the bedroom, displays give information about Shakespeare's family tree, career and business affairs. Notice the original architectural features of the house: heavy oak beams from the Forest of Arden and well-worn floorboards. The living room and kitchen on the ground floor are furnished just as they would have been in Shakespeare's time, and the lovely gardens behind the house are planted with trees and flowers mentioned in Shakespeare's works.

Scholars doing research in Shakespeariana use the library and archives of the **Shakespeare Centre,** next door to the Birthplace. Built by private subscription from the United States and Canada, the Centre is the headquarters of the Shakespeare Birthplace Trust and hosts exhibitions on Shakespearean subjects. Before you pay the small fee to see the current show, look over the Shakespearean characters etched in the glass panels of

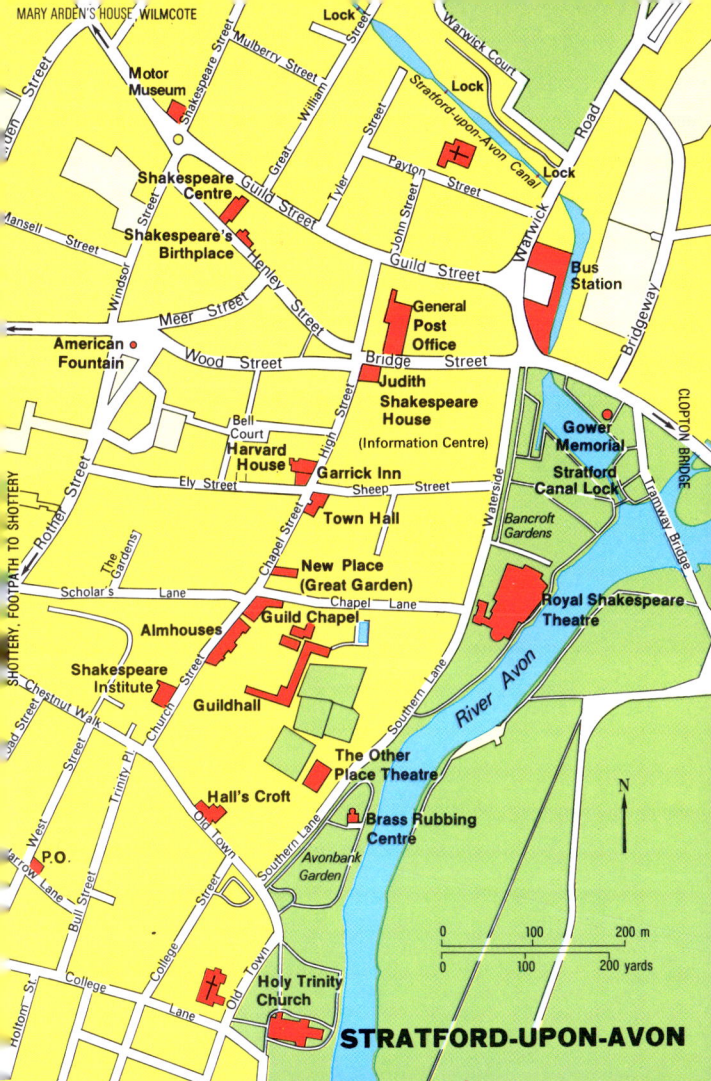

MARY ARDEN'S HOUSE, WILMCOTE

Lock

Warwick Court

Lock

Stratford-upon-Avon Canal

Lock

Motor Museum

Shakespeare Centre

Shakespeare's Birthplace

Payton Street

Bus Station

Guild Street

American Fountain

Meer Street

Wood Street

General Post Office

Bridge Street

Judith Shakespeare House

(Information Centre)

FOOTPATH TO SHOTTERY

Bell Court

Harvard House

Garrick Inn

Sheep Street

Gower Memorial

Stratford Canal Lock

Bancroft Gardens

Waterside

Ely Street

Town Hall

The Gardens

Scholar's Lane

New Place (Great Garden)

Chapel Lane

Almhouses

Guild Chapel

Royal Shakespeare Theatre

River Avon

Shakespeare Institute

Guildhall

Chestnut Walk

Southern Lane

The Other Place Theatre

Hall's Croft

Brass Rubbing Centre

Avonbank Garden

Trinity Pl.

Old Town

Southern Lane

West Street

P.O.

Narrow Lane

Bull Street

N

0   100   200 m

0   100   200 yards

College Lane

Holy Trinity Church

STRATFORD-UPON-AVON

the vestibule by a distinguished English craftsman.

At the corner of Bridge and High streets stands another house once occupied by a Shakespeare. **Judith Shakespeare House,** now the town's Tourist Information Centre, was the home of William Shakespeare's daughter, who married one Thomas Quiney, a wine merchant by trade.

Walk a short distance along High Street to the venerable, half-timbered Garrick Inn—

one of Stratford's most congenial pubs today, as it probably was four centuries ago. Right next door is **Harvard House,** another half-timbered structure rich in ingenious woodcarving. Thomas Rogers, a prosperous butcher and alderman, rebuilt the house after a disastrous fire in 1596. Meticulously restored in the early part of this century, it survives as one of the finest period houses in town. Thomas Rogers' daughter, Katherine, married

Robert Harvard of Southwark, and had a son John, who was educated at Cambridge and then went on to Cambridge, Massachusetts, where he helped to found Harvard University.

Stratford's handsome **Town Hall,** begun in 1767, stands at the corner of Chapel and Sheep streets. It dates from a time of renewed interest in Shakespeare's art and took pride of place at the Jubilee celebration of 1769. The actor

Foul weather or fair, enthusiasts flock to Shakespeare's Birthplace.

David Garrick, organizer, tireless promoter and main beneficiary of the Jubilee, donated the bust of Shakespeare which is set high on the wall in Sheep Street. Before the Jubilee, an earlier town hall had served as a theatre for itinerant troupes of players performing Shakespearean works.

51

William Shakespeare's fine brick-and-timber house, New Place (once at the corner of Chapel Street and Chapel Lane), survived its illustrious owner by two centuries. A Reverend Francis Gastrell had bought the house from Shakespeare's descendants, but grew so tired of souvenir hunters and heavy taxes that he set it on fire in a fit of pique. All that remains is Great Garden, a pleasant place for a rest.

New Place Museum, next door on Chapel Street, houses the collection of Roman and Saxon artefacts that belonged to Shakespeare's granddaughter, Elizabeth Hall Nash, and her husband Thomas Nash. The charming, gabled house, beautifully restored to its Tudor state, is as fascinating as the objects it contains.

From Roman times through the medieval centuries to its flowering in the age of Elizabeth I, Stratford's rich and colourful history is outlined in the exhibition rooms. Mementoes of the Shakespeare Jubilee of 1769 abound, providing a backward glance at the history of Shakespearean tourism.

Many other Stratford buildings have links with the town's most famous son. On Church Street near the corner of Chapel Lane is the **Guildhall,** which houses the Grammar School where young Will is thought to have studied. The quaint half-timbered, two-storey structure was raised in 1417 for the town's Guild of the Holy Cross, a religious order. John Shakespeare, as a city official, would have been entitled to send his son to the school free of charge, and it's thought very probable that William occupied one of the stout wooden school desks, though no records survive to confirm it. School children still attend classes here, so visitors are allowed inside only during school holidays.

The **Chapel of the Guild of the Holy Cross,** connected to the Guildhall in the 1400s, now serves as the school's chapel. Notice the quaint mural of the *Last Judgement,* painted around 1500.

Next to the Guildhall on Church Street are Stratford's **Almshouses,** which have housed some of the town's pensioners since 1427. In earlier times, the Almshouses provided no more than a roof and

Great Garden: where Shakespeare himself looked out on a view of "daisies pied and violets blue".

basic necessities, but today's occupants live in comfort—not to mention style—for the Elizabethan building has been thoroughly modernized inside.

Other venerable buildings in Stratford provide intriguing glimpses of life in Shakespeare's time. **Hall's Croft,** in the street named Old Town, is the most charming and authentic of the Elizabethan houses preserved by the Birthplace Trust. Susanna Shakespeare, daughter of the Bard, lived at Hall's Croft after her marriage to Dr. John Hall. The house is furnished as it would have been when the Halls occupied it 400 years ago. Appropriately, as Dr. Hall was a physician, Tudor surgical implements and medical books are on display upstairs.

A "croft" was an enclosed garden attached to a house, and Hall's Croft boasts a fine one, open to visitors who pay the entry fee to the house. Several rooms have been set aside

William Shakespeare

Though William Shakespeare's talents later took him to London, he always thought of Stratford as his home. He was born in the Warwickshire town on April 23, 1564. His father, John Shakespeare, was a farmer who had moved from the countryside to seek a better life. John turned to glove-making and dealing in wool, and soon grew rich enough to buy the fine house in Henley Street where his son was born.

In 1582, at the age of 19, William married Anne Hathaway, a woman eight years his senior, with whom he had three children. Little is known of his life during the period before he moved to London in the late 1580s. It is likely that he was associated with a theatrical company right from the start.

By the 1590s, Shakespeare's career as a playwright was well on its way. Success brought prosperity as well as fame, and in 1597 the poet bought a grand house in Stratford and named it New Place. He also owned shares in the company that built the famous Globe Theatre in London two years later.

During the last years of his life, Shakespeare was regarded as England's foremost dramatist. He spent most of his time in Stratford and died here on April 23, 1616, at the age of 52. Seven years later, when Shakespeare's plays were first published, admirers became curious about the Bard's native town and the region that inspired his work. The Stratford phenomenon had begun.

On display at Hall's Croft: implements of the physician's art. Shakespeare as he is remembered.

for the Hall's Croft Festival Club, a social and cultural centre. Although the lounge, reading rooms and budget-priced luncheon restaurant are open only to members, anyone can join. Ask the attendant in the lounge for information about the inexpensive short-term membership.

Though it was in London that Shakespeare worked, he remained attached to Stratford all his life. He died here in 1616, and was buried in **Holy Trinity Church** on Trinity Street. A visit to his tomb in the chancel, marked by a simple stone slab, is an obligatory stop for literary pilgrims to Stratford.

After visiting the tomb, look for the ranks of choir stalls carved in dark wood. As in most churches of the time, each stall has a seat that could be tipped up when it was necessary to stand during a service. The services were long in those days, so the undersides of the seats were fitted with brackets called misericords, which could support worshippers while they were standing. Each misericord is carved with a vignette of Stratford daily life. There are a few religious subjects, but most are humorous scenes meant to draw a chuckle.

The oldest part of the church, the Chapel of St. Thomas à Becket, was dedicated in 1331. Memorials to Hugh Clopton and his family, Stratford's most illustrious citizens in the generation before Shakespeare, abound. The American Window, showing the *Adoration of the Magi*, casts soft colours on St. Peter's Chapel. It was donated to the church in 1896 by the people of the United States.

Stratford's Tudor monuments are a vivid reminder of Shakespeare's time, but without doubt the most important memorial to the Bard is the **Royal Shakespeare Theatre.** There's no better way to reach it than through the lovely Avonbank Garden, just north of Holy Trinity Church. The garden, open to all for a riverside stroll, harbours a stone summerhouse which now serves as a brass-rubbing centre.

The memorial theatre of 1879 that stood at the foot of Chapel Lane by the River Avon was burned to the ground in 1926. Today's substantial red-brick theatre opened for its first performance in 1932. Come in the evening for a play (the standard is first-rate), or sit in the cafeteria or the riverside res-

A Stratford idyll: drifting downstream on the Avon for another view of town.

taurant, wrapped in Shakespearean thought as the Avon flows silently by.

The RST, entered from Waterside, has its own Picture Gallery and Museum, a treasure-house of Shakespeariana. Portraits of famous actors (some by great painters), displays of costumes and sets, and relics of the theatre's past give an idea of Stratford's theatre history.

The beautiful **Bancroft Gardens** lie north of the RST between Waterside and the Avon, up to the Canal Wharf and Lock. The old canal lock, leaky as ever, is still in service. Two bridges cross the Avon here—the old Tramway, a relic of the earliest railways in Britain (now reserved for pedestrians) and the venerable Clopton, which carries vehicles, as it has for centuries.

To the west of the bridges is the **Gower Memorial** to Shakespeare, cast in Paris in 1888. The Bard is enthroned in great dignity, while a memorable character from each type

57

of drama stands beneath his pedestal: Hamlet represents Philosophy; Lady Macbeth, Tragedy; Prince Hal, History; and Falstaff, Comedy. The monument couldn't be in a better spot. Mary Arden probably walked by this place as she came from neighbouring Wilmcote for her wedding with John Shakespeare, and William must have crossed Clopton Bridge every time he returned from London.

The most photographed of Shakespearean landmarks is undoubtedly **Anne Hathaway's Cottage,** which lives up to its world-wide reputation for picturesque charm. The cottage—actually a farmhouse which was large for its time—is in the village of SHOTTERY, a pleasant 15-minute stroll from Stratford along the well-marked footpath that begins at Evesham Place. There's also a bus service to Shottery from Bridge Street or the American Fountain.

Shakespeare and his wife, Anne Hathaway, lived in Stratford; but the Hathaway cottage continued to be owned by the Hathaway family until 1892. It was bought for preservation in that year, and with the house came some of the furnishings left from Anne's time.

Enter the cottage through the garden, bright with the colour and scent of roses. The thatched, half-timbered farmhouse is well preserved despite extensive repairs after a fire in 1969. Each thatched roof lasts about 25 years with only minor repairs and weighs almost 12 tons.

The staff are eager to explain the workings of the ovens and other antique features. Among the 16th-century furnishings in the house is Anne Hathaway's bed, which may just be the one Shakespeare bequeathed to her by this enigmatic sentence in his will: "I gyve vnto my wief my second best bed…".

The last of the buildings included in the Birthplace Trust is **Mary Arden's House** in WILMCOTE, 3 miles north-west of Stratford. If the weather is good, nothing could be more pleasant than the 40-minute walk to Wilmcote along the towpath of Stratford Canal.

Mary Arden, William Shakespeare's mother, lived in the quaint, rambling farmhouse in Wilmcote before her marriage. The Ardens were successful farmers. The large dovecote next to the house was an Elizabethan status symbol, as only the wealthiest farmers built them. The Arden property remained a working farm until the 1930s and has changed little over the centuries. Surrounded by sheds and barns which now house a farming museum, Mary Arden's house is alive with the spirit of country life.

The furnishings which you see in the house would have been a familiar sight to Mary herself. When Mary's father died in 1556, a complete list of the house's contents was compiled. Though the furnishings were dispersed when Mary married John Shakespeare in 1557, the list survived. It provided the key to authentic restoration.

Shakespeare Country

Beyond Stratford lie the verdant fields and forests of Warwickshire, dotted with tidy villages, imposing manor houses and historic castles. It's surprising to discover that the landscape hasn't changed very much in the four centuries since Shakespeare wrote:

I know a bank where the wild thyme blows,
Where oxlips and the nodding violet grows,
Quite over-canopi'd with luscious woodbine,
With sweet musk-roses and with eglantine.

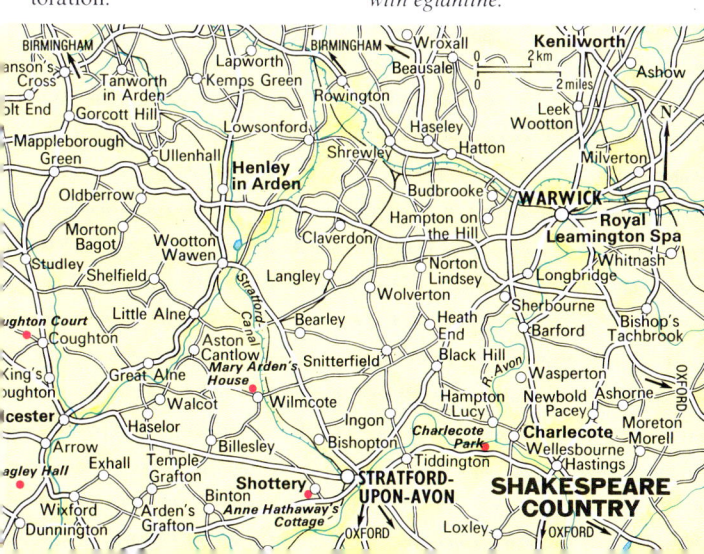

To see the countryside at its most beautiful, travel by car or bicycle. Bus services are good, but they usually keep to the highways, instead of following the more scenic secondary roads.

🏃 Charlecote Park

The River Avon winds a few miles through flat meadowland to Charlecote Park, a stately Elizabethan mansion surrounded by a vast deer park. According to legend, young Will Shakespeare was caught poaching deer here, though historians assure us it wasn't so. Today the estate (the property of the Lucy fam-ily for 700 years) and the red brick 16th-century house are preserved by the National Trust.

Major alterations were made to Charlecote in the 19th century by George and Mary Elizabeth Lucy, and only the gatehouse looks as it did when Queen Elizabeth I visited in 1572. Elsewhere, the popular Elizabethan Revival style of the Victorian era prevails. Portraits of Lucy ancestors from eight centuries of family history look down from every wall,

Scenes of country life: thatched cottage, stately Charlecote Park.

and motifs from the Lucy coat-of-arms—pike fish, boar's head and little crosses—appear throughout the house.

Most of the antique furniture was collected by George Lucy and his wife: tables of polished stone, Boulle cabinets (of inlaid tortoiseshell), classical vases and lapis lazuli candle-holders. The tremendous carved oak Charlecote sideboard, the work of a school of woodcarvers that flourished in Warwickshire in the mid-1800s, is typical of Elizabethan Revival work. Scenes from the reign of Queen Elizabeth I crowd every available inch of space.

Several miles north of Charlecote, across the River Avon, is the village of HAMPTON LUCY. There's a fine Gothic Revival church, attractive thatched houses and an inviting pub.

Warwick

A picturesque road connects Charlecote with the pretty town of Warwick, about 8 miles to the north-east. As you enter town through the West Gate, you pass the gabled Elizabethan **Lord Leycester Hospital**. The buildings, the finest of the period in Warwick, were converted into a rest home for old soldiers by

Robert Dudley, Earl of Leicester, Queen Elizabeth I's favourite. One of the residents will show you around the old chapel, kitchen and banqueting hall.

The **Collegiate Church of St. Mary** in North Gate Street was damaged by fire in 1694, but the present Gothic Revival building contains the original 12th-century crypt and 14th-century choir. The alabaster tombs of Thomas Beauchamp, Earl of Warwick, and his wife lie in the chancel. Beauchamp, a warrior at Poitiers and a commander at Crécy—the two great English victories in the Hundred Years' War—died in 1369.

The magnificent 15th-century **Beauchamp chapel** also survived the fire. In the centre stands the gleaming gilt bronze tomb of Richard Beauchamp, the captor and Chief Inquisitor of Joan of Arc. Robert Dudley and his third wife, Lettice, are entombed in polychrome marble. The legs of Dudley's effigy are made of iron, though they appear to be of stone. Robert's older brother, Ambrose

Dudley, Earl of Warwick, lies nearby.

Warwick Castle dominates the town from a steep cliff beside the Avon. Peacocks strut and squawk around the extensive gardens, lofty towers guard the curtain wall, and the dungeon is well equipped with torture chambers. The present Earl of Warwick still resides at the castle.

The first fortifications were primitive earthworks raised by the daughter of Alfred the Great in 914 as protection against Danish raiding parties. The 14th-century gatehouse, most of the towers and the formidable walls were built by the Beauchamps, the wealthy and powerful medieval earls of Warwick. Shakespeare described one of them as a "proud setter-up and puller-down of kings". The Water Gate Tower contains the room of Sir Fulke Greville, the earl who was murdered by his valet in 1628. Sir Fulke's ghost is said to haunt the place to this day.

The **state apartments** retain all the splendour of their 17th- and 18th-century decoration: lacquer panelling, gilding and richly carved woodwork, brocades, crystal chandeliers and sumptuous carpets. A celebrated equestrian portrait of

Still in splendid shape, Lord Leycester Hospital is a showpiece of Elizabethan architecture.

Charles I by Van Dyck and a painting of two lions by Rubens hang in the living room. A focal point of the Great Hall, restored to baronial splendour after a fire in 1871, is the Kenilworth buffet. This massive oak sideboard, like the one at Charlecote, was carved by Warwickshire craftsmen in the mid-19th century. The scenes recall Queen Elizabeth I's visit to Kenilworth Castle. A fine collection of paintings is displayed in the Ladies' Day Room, including works by Holbein, Pieter de Hooch, Van Dyck and others.

West to Alcester

One of the prettiest drives from Stratford winds 10 miles through bucolic panoramas of grazing cattle, neat stone fences and gnarled English oaks to **Ragley Hall,** the beautiful 17th-century Palladian mansion of the Marquess and Marchioness of Hertford. "Capability" Brown laid out the 400-acre park, and the house was designed in 1680 by Robert Hooke, a contemporary of Wren. Fine 18th-century furniture, silver and porcelain can be seen. There are many superb paintings by Reynolds, especially in the Green Drawing Room. And

the enormous Great Hall has exquisite baroque decorations: Corinthian pilasters, moulded cornices, huge fireplaces and a painting of *Britannia* on the ceiling.

The landmarks of nearby ALCESTER (pronounced Awlster) are the quaint houses along Butter Lane, the town hall of 1641 and the Parish Church of St. Nicholas.

North of Alcester stands **Coughton Court,** ancestral home of the Throckmorton

Warwick Castle, set high on a hill, was well supplied with all the requisites of medieval warfare—dungeons, torture chambers and the like.

family since 1409. The Throckmortons, who were Roman Catholic, suffered many privations during the civil war, but their house has survived in all its splendour.

The grand gatehouse dates from early Tudor times, and the two Gothic Revival wings preserve half-timbering from the time of Queen Elizabeth I.

Relics of the Catholic Stuarts are displayed in the house, as well as portraits of countless Throckmortons. You'll be shown the so-called priestholes constructed by this pious family. They're passageways that lead to secret hiding places, where the Catholic clergy could be protected from persecution.

65

The Cotswolds

The thatched cottages of Shakespeare Country soon merge into the handsome stone houses of the Cotswold Hills (scarcely more than ripples and bumps, in fact). A farmer called Cod settled here in Saxon times and the hills around his property became known as "Cod's Wolds". The name later came to include the area covered by the range of hills from Chipping Campden to Bath, and from Cheltenham to Burford.

Farming the thin topsoil was difficult, and agriculture was abandoned in the 13th century in favour of sheep-raising. Merchants grew rich in the wool and cloth trades, spending their money building magnificent "wool churches" and country estates. Decline in the wool trade in the 19th century brought an end to prosperity, but poverty was a blessing in disguise. The picturesque Cotswold Hills were barely touched by the Industrial Revolution, and today villagers earn their living from tourism, rather than trade or industry.

Though just about any itinerary chosen inevitably means coming across one or another of the area's attractions, the circular tour we propose from Moreton-in-Marsh covers all the highlights: Chipping Campden, Broadway, Cheltenham, Cirencester, Fairford, Bourton-on-the-Water, as well as Stow-on-the-Wold. The ideal way to travel is by car, making short excursions by bicycle or on foot. Trains and frequent bus services link the major towns, often only a few miles apart. For full schedules, consult the Cotswold Bus and Rail Guide, published by the Gloucestershire County Council.

Moreton-in-Marsh

Moreton-in-Marsh (a corruption of "march" or boundary), a "newcomer" among Cotswold towns, was founded by the Abbot of Westminster in 1226. The town's High Street incorporates part of an old Roman highway known as the Fosse Way (now covered by the A429). From Moreton, the road ran straight as an arrow along the western boundary ("march") of Roman Britain to Cirencester.

Although Moreton flourished in the 14th- and 15th-century days of busy wool-trading, most of the town's charming stone buildings date from the 1600s or later. Houses, shops, inns and pubs were set well back from the High Street, so there's plenty of room for the

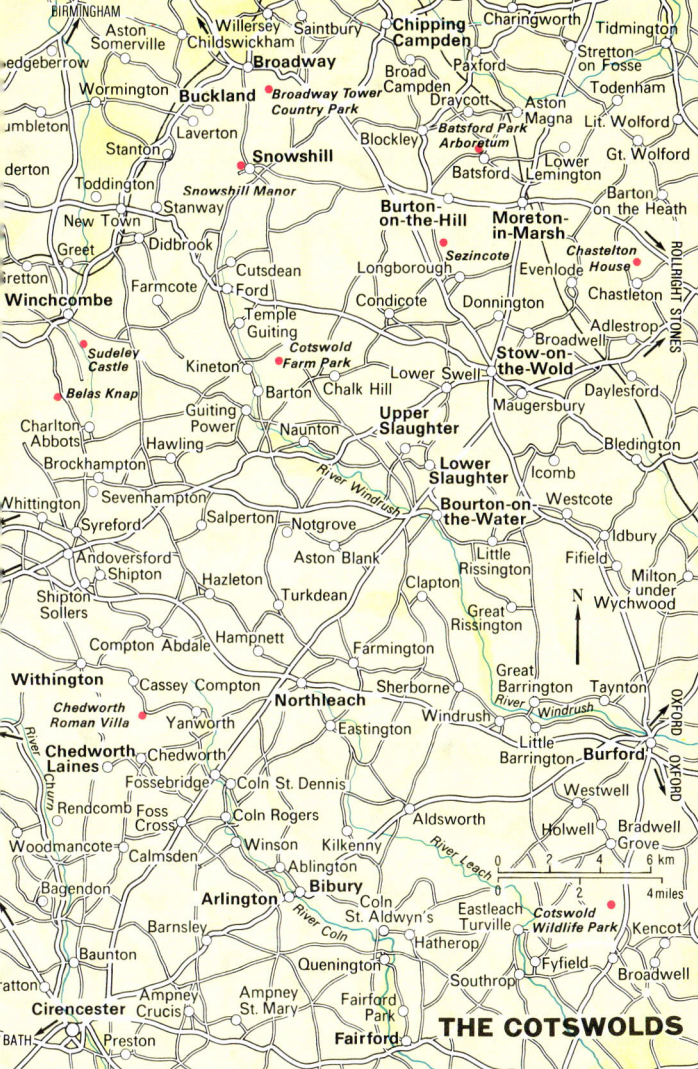

THE COTSWOLDS

Cotswold Stone

Quarries in the Cotswold Hills have provided stone for such buildings as Windsor Castle, Oxford's colleges, Blenheim Palace and the Stratford Town Hall. To preserve architectural unity, Cotswold village houses are still built with the honey-coloured granular limestone.

Cotswold stone is cut and carefully seasoned by weathering. A good mason can tell at a glance whether a certain block of stone is soft or hard, good for building or for carving, and even from which quarry it was cut.

The golden stone enhances the quaint charm of Chipping Campden (left).

big Tuesday market. In earlier times, market fees and taxes were paid at the **Curfew Tower,** the quaint structure beside the petrol station. On top of the tower is the curfew bell, dated 1633. For centuries, its sturdy stone walls served as the town prison.

Redesdale Hall, across High Street from the tower, looks much older than it is. Actually, the stately Renaissance-style residence was built in 1887. The plan is very similar to the old community halls found in many Cotswold towns: the ground floor is an open arcade and there's a large hall on the upper floor.

There's plenty to see in the area around Moreton. You may want to visit **Sezincote**, a Regency house in the Indian style, about a mile west of town. The oriental water garden was created by the famous landscape gardener, Humphry Repton. **Chastleton House** (4 miles to the south-east) is noted for its 17th-century plasterwork and period décor. The topiary garden, designed in 1700, is one of England's oldest.

From Chastleton, a short detour of about 5 miles takes you to the village of LITTLE COMPTON and the nearby **Rollright Stones,** monolithic stone circles erected in the Bronze Age as a place of worship. Local legend long claimed that the grotesque monoliths were men who had been turned to stone, and the circles are still known as the "King's Men" and the "Whispering Knights".

BATSFORD, a village about a mile to the north of Moreton, is accessible by public footpath. The tiny church contains the tombs of the local gentry, and **Batsford Park Arboretum** boasts a wide variety of rare trees, many of them oriental species.

Chipping Campden

Continue a few miles over the hills past Batsford to Chipping Campden, an old market ("chipping") town of gabled stone cottages. Visit the picturesque timber-roofed **Market Hall,** centrepiece of the town's market square since 1627. Its stone floor has been worn to an undulating unevenness over the centuries. The old market cross stands nearby.

Chipping Campden's woolstaplers (dealers in wool) were among the richest men in England during the 14th and 15th centuries. They bought their fleece at **Woolstaplers' Hall,** an interesting old building of 1340 that serves as the town's tourist information bureau and local history museum. In its safekeeping are hundreds of relics from the town's past, as well as many modern exhibits.

Wool money paid for Chipping Campden's **Parish Church of St. James,** another impressive Perpendicular-style building. It's the architectural highlight of this quaint, sleepy town. Brass plaques in the floor of the chancel commemorate the town's prosperous wool merchants, among them William Grevel and his wife, pillars of Chipping Campden's medieval community.

Sir Baptist Hicks, the town's generous 17th-century benefactor, possessed such enormous wealth that he could loan money to King James I and his court. Look for Sir Baptist's ornate black-and-white marble tomb in Gainsborough Chapel. Near him lie Sir Edward Noel and Juliana Hicks Noel, his son-in-law and daughter. They're shown leaping from their tomb in a stony rehearsal for Judgement Day.

The entrance to the churchyard and the "oriental" gateway to Campden House, once Sir Baptist Hicks' estate, stand side by side; the great house was built in 1613, only to be destroyed 30 years later during the civil war. The gateway, banqueting house and garden pavilions are all that remain. Just down the hill from Campden House is a row of gabled almshouses—one of Sir Baptist's more conspicuous good works.

Broadway

From Chipping Campden, head south-west 10 miles in the direction of Broadway. Shortly before the town, stop off at **Broadway Tower Country Park** (just off the A44 highway) for the panoramic view of the Cotswold Hills, scattered with flocks of sheep and herds of cattle and dotted with old villages. Signs near the Gloucestershire-Worcestershire boundary point the way to the park entrance.

Broadway Tower, a "folly", was built in 1799 by the Earl of Coventry for no earthly reason beyond his wife's pleasure. In keeping with the whimsical traditions of the place, the tower was later put to use as a printing shop by the eccentric Broadway book collector, Sir Thomas Phillipps. There are picnic tables nearby.

Life continues at unhurried pace in Broadway, hub of the Cotswolds.

The famous Cotswold town of **Broadway** nestles in the valley below. The lords of Pershore Abbey founded the town in 1251, and its market soon brought in the wealth of the countryside. Broadway enjoyed quiet prosperity until the 19th century, but economic decline did nothing to spoil its charm. Rather the contrary; if anything, it is too much like a picture postcard. The Pre-Raphaelite artists and writers escaped to Broadway from the bustle and intrigues of London, but news of their rural holiday retreat spread, and sightseers followed in the artists' footsteps.

Broadway still hosts great numbers of visitors (so great, parking becomes a problem), who come for the day to enjoy the **High Street,** lined with fine Tudor houses. Renowned for its pleasant restaurants, antique shops and art galleries, Broadway is the kind of place that invites leisurely browsing, shopping and nostalgic thoughts. One of the outstanding buildings is the **Lygon Arms Inn,** headquarters at different times during the civil war for both Charles I and Oliver Cromwell.

Across the fields to the south-west is the tiny hamlet of BUCKLAND, with a smattering of houses and barns. The **Church of St. Michael,** a distinguished Perpendicular structure, has a beautiful 15th-century stained-glass window. Its rectory was built before 1480, and some claim it's the oldest still standing in England. An attractive manor house completes this classic picture of Cotswold village life.

Winchcombe

Continue a short distance past the village of SNOWSHILL to **Snowshill Manor,** which belonged to Winchcombe Abbey in the 9th century. The present house was built around 1500 and enlarged a century later. It subsequently fell into disrepair and was restored only after it became the property of Charles Wade, an eccentric collector with magpie instincts. On display is an incredible clutter of objects that range from Chinese lacquered cabinets to Japanese samurai armour, African musical instruments and old craftsmen's tools. A 20th-century romantic, Mr. Wade read by lamplight and worked at various traditional crafts. His ideals and way of life continue to have a strong appeal, and every year visitors flock to Snowshill, a National Trust property since 1951.

Brass Rubbing

In medieval and Renaissance times, English knights and rich merchants were buried in places of honour beneath the chancels of parish churches. Finely engraved brass plaques bearing images of the departed worthies were placed over their tombs as memorials. Today these plaques are much admired works of art, and they've given rise to the hobby of brass rubbing.

All you need to make a beautiful and lasting souvenir is a large piece of sturdy paper, a big wax crayon and the permission of church authorities, who may charge a small fee. Simply cover the plaque with paper and rub away.

The design of brasses in the 14th and 15th centuries was stereotyped. The dead, their faces devoid of any expression, are shown in ceremonial repose. Of particular interest among later brasses are those in Oxford's college chapels. Many were engraved with views of the colleges or a variety of symbolic scenes.

Centres for brass-rubbing, which have exact replicas of authentic memorial brasses, have sprung up in many places, including Oxford, Stratford and Cirencester. Here you can buy supplies and make rubbings of the replicas.

In a green and wooded valley a few miles on stands **Winchcombe.** Its half-timbered houses date from the 16th century, when the village prospered from tobacco-growing. Although the town was the capital of the powerful Saxon kingdom of Mercia, only the ruins of an abbey founded by King Kenulf remain. Today, artists and artisans have settled in Winchcombe, making it a centre of creative activity, with excellent craft shops, plus a railway museum. The Perpendicular parish church is noted for its grotesque carvings.

In fact, most people only pass through Winchcombe on their way to stately **Sudeley Castle,** on the south-east outskirts of town. King Ethelred the Unready and his heirs were the estate's first owners. In the 15th century, the property was awarded to Sir Ralph Boteller, an admiral in the Hundred Years' War, who built the magnificent castle. Sudeley's hour of glory came in Tudor times, when Henry VIII's widow, Katherine Parr, married Thomas Seymour, lord of Sudeley. Her cosy bedroom with its carved wood panelling has been redecorated as it might have been when she herself occupied it. Queen Elizabeth I visited the castle on several occasions, but the Banqueting Hall where she was entertained so magnificently stands in ruins, destroyed along with the chapel and Katherine Parr's tomb in the civil war. Restoration of the castle was undertaken in the 19th century by Sir Gilbert Scott, who also designed the ornate monument to Katherine Parr in the chapel.

In addition to such historic mementoes as Katherine Parr's prayer book and one of her love letters to Thomas Seymour, Sudeley boasts a fine collection of paintings by Zucchero, Turner and Constable.

The Emma Dent collection of Victorian autographs, letters and photographs helps make historical figures come to life. There's also a costume exhibition and a display of flints and pottery from Belas Knap, a Stone Age barrow $1\frac{1}{2}$ miles from the castle.

East of Sudeley at the **Cotswold Farm Park** (near Guiting Power), pets and baby farm animals are kept, many of them rare and ancient livestock breeds. Look for the "Cotswold lions", a kind of sheep, and "Iron Age" cattle.

The band plays on at Sudeley.

Cheltenham

The city of Cheltenham, hub for the western Cotswolds, stands at the junction of several major highways and on a direct rail line to London. Now a busy town, it began urban life in 1715, when an alkaline spring was discovered on the banks of the River Chelt. It developed as a spa town, and visits by Dr. Johnson, Handel, King George III and the Duke of Wellington (who was cured of a liver complaint) brought Cheltenham fame and fortune. During the Regency period early in the 19th century, a new town plan was designed, creating wide, tree-shaded avenues and plenty of parks, gardens and promenades for taking exercise—an important part of the cure. Nowadays, most of the spa buildings are closed or converted to other uses, but you can still enjoy Cheltenham's Regency architecture and cool, leafy walks.

Start your tour of the town at the **Promenade,** Cheltenham's main shopping thoroughfare, lined with terraced buildings that now serve as Municipal Offices but were private residences during Cheltenham's Regency heyday. Just off the Promenade are the **Imperial Gardens** and **Town Hall,** a venue for concerts during the Cheltenham Music Festival in July. A fountain here still dispenses the famous mineral water.

Continue up the hill past the Grecian-style Queen's Hotel (completed in 1838, a year after Queen Victoria came to the throne) to **Montpellier Walk,** with its small shops. The caryatids (sculpted female bearer figures) between them are a highlight of the town's elegant Regency architecture. At the bottom of the Walk stands the **Montpellier Rotunda,** yet another fine example of the Regency style. The Pantheon in Rome provided the model for the dome of this former "pump room", where spa water was taken.

The **Pittville Pump Room,** a gracious Grecian building set in a beautiful park a mile to the north of the city centre remains open as a tourist attraction. Anyone can try the cure—some mineral water from the elaborate well-head and a brisk stroll through the spa gardens.

From Cheltenham's bustling streets, follow country roads about 3 miles to WITHINGTON. It's only a short distance from here to the extensive remains of **Chedworth Roman Villa,** a lavish country estate occupied from the 2nd to 4th centuries

A.D. by prosperous Roman landholders. The sumptuous mansion, hidden in the depths of a dense evergreen forest, now seems improbably remote. But the Fosse Way ran only a few miles to the east.

Excavations carried out shortly after the discovery of the villa in 1864 exposed the north and west wings to view. The walls no longer extend to their original height, but you can still marvel at the sophisticated plan, the central heating and sewage systems and elaborate bath complex. Today the National Trust cares for the villa and its mosaics, including the exquisite pavement of the four seasons that covered the heated floor of the dining room. A small museum houses artefacts unearthed on the site: coins, iron tools, figures of Roman deities, and so on.

The Cirencester Area

Roman landholders lived in luxury at Chedworth, but not in isolation. Just a few miles away at **Cirencester,** the ancient Roman town of Corinium Dobunnorum, was the largest Romano-British city after London. Today there are few reminders of Roman occupation in the "capital" of the Cotswolds. Anglo-Saxon warriors sacked the city in the 6th century, obliterating the grid-like town plan of the Romans. Only the amphitheatre (southwest of the city centre) and a few sections of the Roman wall (revealed in 1963 excavations) escaped destruction.

For a vivid picture of Cirencester's eventful past, visit the well-organized **Corinium Museum** in Park Street. Displays of local finds from Roman times, including beautiful mosaic pavements and a reconstruction of a mosaic craftsman's workshop, give an idea of the high standard of living that prevailed in Roman Britain.

Cirencester Park, the stately house of the Earl of Bathurst, to the west of the museum, luxuriates in extensive grounds. The park, with its footpaths, picnic sites and polo centre—the scene of lively matches in summer—remains open to the public year-round.

Of all Cirencester's architectural glories, none is greater than its Perpendicular "wool church", the **Parish Church of St. John the Baptist,** in Market Place at the centre of town. Originally a Saxon church stood here, but in 1117 Henry I began a new building in the Norman style. Cotswold wool

Bird's-eye view of Cirencester, a lively town since Roman times.

magnates later embellished the king's creation until it was one of the finest and largest parish churches in England. Rich in beautiful brass memorials and 16th-century stained-glass, the church also holds valuable plate, including a decorated gold cup made for the luckless Queen Anne Boleyn in 1535.

To survey the town, climb some 200 steps to the top of the church's pinnacled tower. A few hundred yards to the north, you'll see the ruins of a 12th-century Augustinian abbey, destroyed during the reign of Henri VIII, and a section 30 feet long of Cirencester's Roman wall.

After Cirencester, the next important Cotswold centre is **Fairford,** a small market town 9½ miles to the east. Wool merchant John Tame and his son Edmund financed the **Parish Church of St. Mary,** another outstanding Perpendicular "wool church", between 1490 and 1530. John Tame's tomb rests in the chancel. The great stories of Christianity from the Creation to the Last Judgement come to life in the splendid array of 500-year-old stained-glass windows. And the carvings in wood and stone are no less magnificent, especially the grotesque figures on the outside walls.

Farther east, at the **Cotswold Wildlife Park** ($9^{1}/_{2}$ miles from Fairford), African gazelles, zebras and rhinos roam the hills. A small zoo stocked with monkeys, leopards and pandas adds to the appeal of this popular tourist attraction.

Less than 1,000 people inhabit the sleepy little village of **Bibury,** just north-west of Fairford. Its church dates back to Saxon times, though the Normans and their successors made many changes. In the adjoining graveyard, the tombs of the local wool merchants all bear stylized representations of wool sacks—a potent symbol of wealth and prosperity in the medieval Cotswolds. Down the hill from the village proper, along the River Coln, stand the picturesque houses of **Arlington Row,** constructed as a textile factory three centuries ago.

A farm museum has been created a stone's throw away, at the **Arlington Mill Museum.** Vintage wooden and metal machines such as you'll see here spared many an agricultural labourer an aching back in the days before the Age of Industry. Displays of steam toys and Victorian costume round out the exhibition, installed in Bibury's 17th-century corn mill. The Bibury Trout Farm, though a commercial establishment, welcomes visitors. View the dozens of trout pools, feed the fish—or stock up on today's dinner.

Go north-west again a few miles to **Northleach,** another town that prospered during the wool era. Its splendid Perpendicular church, a favourite haunt of brass-rubbers, rivals those in Chipping Campden and Cirencester. Copies from Northleach's superb brass plaques of wool merchants are prized souvenirs. Make your own with paper and crayons from a shop in the market square. Look for the monument to John Fortey, whose wealth paid for the nave with its vaulted roof and the window above the chancel arch that makes the interior so airy.

Think Roman as you travel

north-east to **Bourton-on-the-Water,** a pretty town 5 miles away on the River Windrush. Bourton grew so prosperous in Roman times that for centuries ancient coins were dredged from the river by amateur archaeologists. The Windrush flows, silent and beautiful, right through the centre of town, and low-arched footbridges of mellow Cotswold stone straddle the stream.

Bourton boasts the most extensive and eclectic collection of tourist attractions in the Cotswolds. There's a Motor Museum, Aquarium, and Model Railway, not to mention an old mill, parish church, and Model Village— an impressive scale model of Bourton itself. The odd parrot or macaw winging its way over the village serves as an airborne advertisement for **Birdland,** home of some 600 exotic species. The nature preserve has been created alongside the river in the centre of town. Last but not least comes the Butterfly Exhibition, a creepy-crawly display of live insects and butterflies.

But Bourton's real appeal is the town itself, and the river-

Folk dancers enliven a summer day.

side cafés, restaurants and pubs provide just the place to stop for refreshment before heading on half a mile or so to the Slaughters.

Outwardly, life in LOWER SLAUGHTER hasn't changed very much in centuries. A trout stream flows through this pleasant old village and there's a picturesque manor house (now a hotel) and steepled church. In neighbouring UPPER SLAUGHTER, a farming village with a medieval look, villagers ford the river in the centre of town. The barns have dovecotes built into their walls and agriculture is barely disturbed by the few curious visitors at the village's single hotel.

Your journey through the Cotswolds comes to an end in **Stow-on-the-Wold.** This charming village just northeast of the Slaughters and no more than a ten-minute ride from the starting point in Moreton perches high on a hill at the junction of several important roads. Quaint gabled shops that list crazily to this side or that surround Stow's spacious **market square.** Don't confuse the steepled Town Hall in the square with the nearby Parish Church of St. Edward, a venerable structure begun in Norman times with various later additions.

What to Do

Shopping

Of all the cities in the heart of England, Oxford is probably the best for shopping. The quality and selection of goods available in Broad Street, Queen Street shopping precinct, Cornmarket, the High and, to a lesser extent, Little Clarendon Street is extraordinary for a town its size. Nearby Woodstock has lots of beautiful little shops, as does Cheltenham's Promenade and Montpellier Walk. And there's no better place to buy antiques and hand-crafted items than in the villages of Shakespeare Country and the Cotswolds.

Here are some good buys.

Antiques. England's old country houses, largely untouched by wartime plundering and bombing, disgorge a wealth of treasures onto the antique market. Many a knowledgeable London dealer buys in the country. Check local papers for details of auction sales.

Books. In Oxford, a wide range of subjects is available from the various departments **81**

of Blackwell's, a real institution, in Broad Street. There are all sorts of bookshops scattered round the town, including some that specialize in old or rare editions.

Brass items. Horse brasses—shiny harness medallions—make simple and inexpensive souvenirs. Many people use them as paperweights. The authentic ones—smooth on the back from rubbing against the horse's hide—can be pricey, but attractive modern copies are inexpensive. Brass candlesticks and nutcrackers are also good buys.

China and glass. Choose from a wide range of the best English bone china, Staffordshire figures, Wedgwood objects and lead crystal.

Clothing. Classic woollens for men and women have long been a British speciality. Also look for original dresses in fresh country prints and romantic creations in delicate silks and antique fabrics.

Crafts. Many respected craftsmen have studios in the Cotswolds. Their wares are exhibited and sold in Stratford, Oxford and Cheltenham. Many beautiful items are available, ranging from unusual candles to silver jewellery, wooden toys and hand-tooled leather articles. Winchcombe

and Broadway are particularly noted for their craft shops. In Cirencester, you'll find a large crafts cooperative in the centre of town.

Old prints and maps. Look for prints of Oxford, Stratford and other cities as they used to be, as well as old maps of all the English counties.

Shakespearean souvenirs. Mementoes of a visit to Stratford range from plaster busts of Shakespeare and ceramic replicas of the Birthplace to deluxe editions of the plays.

Prices

In Common Market countries, VAT (value-added tax) is charged on all retail sales. However, shoppers from non-Common Market countries who export a substantial purchase can request a rebate or escape the tax altogether (see p. 120 for details). Not all shops participate in the tax-free scheme; many require that you buy at least a certain pound's worth of goods.

Markets

The weekly markets held in Oxford, Stratford and many Cotswold towns belong to a tradition as old as commerce itself. It's pleasant to shop in the open air, and there's always the possibility of discovering a bargain or an unusual item. Haggling over the price, though not common, may help clinch the deal.

Oxford's weekly market is at Gloucester Green, a 2-minute walk from Cornmarket Street. Stratford is famous for its livestock markets, though most tourists find the general-purpose Rother Market more interesting. The Rother Market is held in the market-place, beside the American Fountain on Fridays. Many Cotswold towns boast ancient market crosses, though nowadays the presence of a cross doesn't always mean that a market is held.

Sports

The English invented most of the sports mentioned here. To this day, they remain inveterate sports enthusiasts, and the area including Oxford, Stratford and the Cotswolds proves no exception. Wherever you go, you'll be able to participate in or watch a wide variety of outdoor activities.

For Spectators

Soccer. Inveterate fans, the English follow local and World Cup play with equal devotion. Some of the professional teams in England's heartland rank among the best in the country. Check local newspapers for details of clubs and match schedules.

Rugby. This popular game originated when a soccer player at the Rugby School picked up the ball and ran with it. Rather than disqualifying him, those present heralded the beginning of a new sport. There's likely to be a top-level game in Cheltenham or Oxford during the season.

Cricket. Although a slow and languid game, cricket is not without its moments of excitement and tension. The uninitiated are bound to be somewhat mystified at first, but the rules aren't hard to

pick up. Just remember that there are two teams of 11 players, both wearing the same white trousers and shirts. The two players on the field holding bats belong to one team, all the others to the second, whose object is to remove the batsmen.

A mood of gentlemanly sportsmanship and an incomparable setting distinguish cricket from many other games. Players in white move across the green grass of the

pitch, perhaps against the backdrop of a parish church. The action is punctuated only by the sporadic, polite applause of the spectators (intent on their sandwiches and tea) and the occasional sound of a crunch as bat hits ball. It's all very civilized in a hectic world.

Horse Events. National Hunt events take place throughout the year in Cheltenham (the venue for the Gold Cup Meeting in March), Stratford, Stow-on-the-Wold and Broadway.

A game for gentlemen: cricket is the quintessential English sport, dignified, sedate and unhurried.

Polo matches are held at Cirencester Park on Sundays in the summer.

Rowing. Each Oxford college has its own boat club and rowing team. Competition reaches fever pitch during Eights Week in May, when the colleges vie to be "Head of the River".

Boating

A superb system of canals remains from the 18th-century heyday of inland water transport. Together with the rivers Thames and Avon and their tributaries, it links the cities of Stratford, Warwick, Banbury and Oxford, among others.

Cruise the region for several days in your own narrowboat (a kind of houseboat), or spend a leisurely half-hour sailing along the Avon from the docks by Stratford's Royal Shakespeare Theatre. Boats depart frequently, and the cost is very reasonable.

In Oxford, try your hand at punting—propelling a special square-ended, flat-bottomed boat with a pole. Punts can be hired on the Thames at Folly Bridge and on the Cherwell at Magdalen Bridge or Bardwell Road.

Bicycling

Oxford, Stratford and the larger towns in the Cotswolds have shops that hire out bicycles (see p. 106). Cycling in England's heartland is a joy, if you observe a few rules. Go cautiously where high hedgerows reduce visibility, especially at corners and along curves. Be sure to keep to the *left* side of the road. And don't ride on the main highways (roads classified with an "A"). Traffic on these thoroughfares is always too heavy and fast for cyclists, and there is no room for two-wheeled traffic.

Walking

It's not surprising that walking is a favourite English pastime. The countryside is exceptionally beautiful, with gently rolling hills and many ancient footpaths, carefully marked by green signposts. For walks in the country, particularly if the weather has been wet, you'll need a pair of sturdy hiking boots. Here are some suggested itineraries:

In Oxford, take Addison's Walk through the Water Meadows by Magdalen College, or enjoy the scenery in Christ Church Meadow. The towpaths along the Cherwell and Thames also make for interesting walking. Other pleasant paths are yours to discover in the spacious grounds of Blenheim Palace.

The most scenic walks in Stratford are to Anne Hathaway's cottage in Shottery and along the River Avon. The Stratford Canal towpath, a

Punting is an Oxford speciality: spend a lazy afternoon afloat on the Thames or the Cherwell.

fine track that leads to Mary Arden's house in Wilmcote, goes on for miles.

The Cotswolds are covered by a network of public footpaths marked by signs. They may be simple short-cuts from one part of a town to another, or long cross-country walks from village to village. The paths are of asphalt, gravel, grass—or, after rain, slippery mud. Some cut right across fields and through herds of cattle and sheep. The 100-mile-long Cotswold Way, from Chipping Campden to Bath, follows the scarp, or ridge, of the hills. A walker's guide to the trail can be purchased in local bookshops.

Other Sports

Tennis is as British as Wimbledon, though the capital has no monopoly on the sport. There are good courts in Oxford and most of the larger towns. You'll also find facilities at some country hotels.

Golf is catered for throughout the region, and courses at Stratford, Cirencester and Broadway accept visiting players. A few country hotels also have courses.

Hikers find plenty of sights to explore in England's heartland.

Fishing for trout is rewarding at Moreton-in-Marsh, Bibury and other Cotswold towns. Hotels in the area can arrange for permits.

Centres for **horse riding** abound in Shakespeare Country and the Cotswolds. You can ride by the day or week; instruction is usually available.

To participate in **hunting**, contact the Warwickshire and West Warwickshire Farmers. Townspeople eagerly follow the hunts on Saturdays in autumn, circling the fields on foot or in cars.

Nightlife

While Oxford and Stratford can't compete with the excitements of London, not everybody is in bed by nine o'clock. One or two of the larger hotels have clubs for dinner and dancing, and private clubs and discos draw the young crowd. Oxford is particularly well supplied with discotheques and folk-music clubs. Art films are shown regularly and both professional and undergraduate theatre flourishes. Undergraduates contribute to Oxford's ample classical music, too, complementing the professional events in the "Music at Oxford" series. Opera companies visit on tour, and the city has a music and theatre venue at St. Paul's, Walton Street.

In Shakespeare Country and the Cotswolds, people are early to bed and early to rise. But you won't be far from a welcoming pub (see pp. 96, 99). Each has its own reputation and regular customers. The regulars will respect your right to privacy, but if you break the ice, you'll soon find yourself chatting to new acquaintances. "Town meets gown" in Oxford's pubs, and there's no better place to get to know the university community.

A pilgrimage to Stratford would be incomplete without a night at the theatre. The Royal Shakespeare Company plays year-round (except February) at the Royal Shakespeare Theatre by the Avon. It's a good idea to book well in advance, since tickets can be hard to come by. Occasionally, returned tickets are available at the box office on the day of a performance.

Equally popular is the Company's small experimental theatre, The Other Place. Plays by authors ancient and modern are presented in a former warehouse a short walk from the RST along Southern Lane. Audiences praise the quality and originality of the performances.

Calendar of Events

Villages and towns in England's heartland hold traditional fêtes and celebrations in July and August. Other special events take place throughout the year.

April
Shakespeare's Birthday
(Stratford-upon-Avon)

The Bard's birthday is commemorated on St. George's Day, April 23rd, or the weekend closest to it. Parades highlight the event.

May
Horse Fair
(Stow-on-the-Wold)

One of two important regional sales held annually.

Sudeley Steam Fair
(Sudeley Castle)

A unique collection of steam engines is displayed during Spring Bank Holiday weekend.

June
Dover's Games
(Chipping Campden)

A local "Olympics" featuring old-fashioned rural sports like "cudgel", combat with short, thick sticks. The games were first held in 1612. The Puritans banned them, as did the Victorians, but the tradition survived nonetheless.

July
Music Festival
(Cheltenham)

This outstanding two-week event is dedicated to the work of contemporary British composers.

August/September
Water Games
(Bourton-on-the-Water)

Townspeople keep cool on Bank Holiday Monday by playing soccer *in* the River Windrush.

September
Festival of Literature
(Cheltenham)

Writers and critics come to Cheltenham throughout the month for conferences and discussions.

October

Horse Fair
(Stow-on-the-Wold)

The second of two colourful yearly sales.

Mop Fair
(Stratford-upon-Avon)

This general fair on October 12th features games, sideshows and amusements. It preserves the name of the annual employment bazaars held in medieval times, when farmers and other employers hired help for the coming year.

November 5th

Guy Fawkes Day

Bonfires and processions all over England commemorate the failure of revolutionary plotters to blow up king and Parliament in 1605.

Dining and Drinks

English cuisine has many strong points—as well as a few peculiarities. The best of English cookery can be ranked justifiably with any other in the world, but it's rarely found in restaurants. All too often you come across meat and vegetables that have been cooked in the same pot for hours, rather than a selection of the traditional dishes.

To sample fine English cooking, you need an invitation to dine at home with a country family, at a "noble estate", or at the High Table of one of Oxford's colleges. At certain college "feasts", banquets of multiple courses, fine food is accompanied by rare wines from extensive and well-stocked cellars. On these occasions, endowments pay the bill.

Breakfast

A classic English breakfast can sustain you until tea time. Fruit juices, cereal with milk or cream, bacon, sausages, eggs, kippers (a kind of

Enjoy authentic English fare in the gracious surroundings of an old coaching inn or pub.

smoked herring), numerous slices of toast with butter and marmalade, and tea or coffee—these aren't the choices, but the courses. Some of England's traditional hotels and inns provide just such a breakfast every morning.

Lunch
After a hearty breakfast, you may want to eat frugally at lunchtime (usually noon to 3 p.m.), especially since tea is only a few hours away. Light lunches are the rule in England, especially in the pubs. If you're trying to economize, remember that pub lunches are still one of Britain's best bargains.

Pub fare is standard throughout the country. Cheese and bread—a hefty slice of good English Cheddar with fresh rolls—make a simple but satisfying meal. Or you can ask for a Ploughman's Lunch—cheese, bread, salad and pickle relish. Some pubs serve such time-honoured dishes as Bubble and Squeak, cooked potatoes and cabbage, fried in the pan until crisp, and Toad-in-the-Hole, sausages baked in batter. For a more filling repast, try Shepherd's Pie, a casserole of minced lamb, carrots and onions topped with mashed potatoes.

Pubs always have fried sausages on hand, as well as Scotch eggs, spheres of deep-fried sausage meat with hard-boiled eggs at the centre, served cold. You may want to sample a Cornish pasty (pronounced PAS-tea), pastry filled with beef, potatoes and onions, or a home-made English pork pie. Warm steak and kidney or chicken and mushroom pies can be very good, but be on your guard against the packaged variety. Pubs also offer cold sliced ham, roast beef, chicken or turkey.

Afternoon Tea
Tea, like so many things English, is regulated by long and honoured tradition. A classic tea begins with two pots, a large one filled with India tea, a smaller one with China tea. Lemon or milk—not cream—is served with tea in England. Three courses follow in easy succession. Delicate little sandwiches of cucumber, cress, tomato, ham or cheese are first. Then come scones (rhymes with "John's"), like American biscuits, or crumpets, muffins with butter, thick cream and fruit jam. Last are the tarts, fruit cakes and biscuits (cookies). After such a tea, you'll be well fortified until a late dinner hour.

In rural England, joints and chops are favourite cuts—and friendly service still counts.

Needless to say, simpler versions of afternoon tea are more common. Normally, strong tea (sometimes with milk and sugar already added) and biscuits are served. If you ask for a "cream tea", you'll be given scones with cream and jam. Thick Cornish cream or the ambrosial Devonshire clotted cream are best, though ordinary whipped cream appears most of the time.

High tea, sometimes mistakenly thought to be a particularly elegant afternoon tea, is just the opposite. It came about as the working man's response to the nobility's dinner. A typical high tea includes the normal selection of biscuits or cakes, plus one hot dish, perhaps eggs and bacon.

Dinner
Restaurants in England's heartland offer a varied cuisine, with a few exotic touches. Although menus sometimes have a pronounced foreign bias, you'll still find many hearty English dishes. Well-cooked local specialities can be found at many charming old inns or rustic eating houses out and around in the countryside.

It's always advisable to make reservations in advance. This is especially important for dinner after the theatre; tables in late-night restaurants are always in brisk demand.

For Starters

Many a traditional meal begins with savoury oxtail soup, a beef broth. Cock-a-leekie soup has a chicken base and lots of leeks. Elver cake, a kind of omelette, combines eggs, fried bacon and baby eels. Potted shrimp, salmon or lampreys are cooked with butter and spices and preserved in jars. Smoked mackerel, salmon or herring can be very good, and tasty country pâté made from pork or fish is an English staple.

Check the list of traditional-type inns on p. 99.

Another good way to sample traditional recipes is to spend a few days on a working farm as a paying guest. To experience the food and atmosphere of medieval England, attend a "historical banquet", perhaps at a stately home.

Authentic Indian, Greek, Chinese, French and Italian dishes can be enjoyed in Oxford, Stratford and several Cotswold towns. Standards are generally high, as many restaurants are operated by naturalized foreigners.

Most restaurants open for dinner from 6.30 to 11 p.m.

Main Courses

Beefeaters will delight in England's classic dish, roast beef and crusty Yorkshire pudding, similar to an American popover. Roast leg of lamb, often served with mint sauce, is a favourite. For hearty flavour, order succulent English pork chops or ham, baked or roasted. Gammon, a cut of ham, is boiled or fried.

In season, you can't go wrong with fresh fish or shellfish, whether salmon, trout, Dover sole, oysters or prawns. **95**

Chicken or turkey (perhaps with a sage stuffing) and duck normally appear on menus; in the game season, wild duck, partridge, grouse and pheasant are added to the list.

Main courses normally are garnished with vegetables—usually green beans, Brussels sprouts, cauliflower and peas—and potatoes, perhaps "chips" (French fried), "creamed" (mashed) or "jacket potatoes" (baked in their skins).

Desserts
The "sweet" may be cake (gâteau), cheesecake, or pudding—a part fruit and part cake mixture dessert, baked or steamed to make it rise and set. Christmas pudding, available during the holiday season, contains beef suet, almonds, raisins, sultanas, candied fruit, carrots and apples. Fruit also figures in "fool", a light confection of whipped cream and fruit of the season. Try delectable gooseberry fool, if you have the chance. Fruit tarts and pies are often glorified with a lavish pouring of thick cream. An English trifle is no trifling matter, but a complex blend of sponge cake, fruit or jam, custard or cream and brandy. Syllabub combines wine, lemon juice and whipped cream.

England's Pubs
"There is nothing which has yet been contrived by man, by which so much happiness is produced as by a good tavern or inn", said Dr. Samuel Johnson in 1776. Even if you don't drink, you'll enjoy the friendly atmosphere of England's taverns or public houses—"pubs" for short. The English relax and grow talkative in pubs. The regulars all know one another, and you may feel as if you're intruding on a family reunion at first.

Most establishments have two separate rooms—the public bar, where locals banter and challenge one another to games of darts, and the saloon bar, an ideal place for a chat. The majority of pubs are "tied houses" affiliated with a particular brewery and serving only that brewery's beer.

Pubs are open only at certain times, usually from 11 or 11.30 a.m. to 2.30 or 3 p.m. and from 5.30 or 6 until 11 or 11.30 p.m. Sunday hours are shorter, from noon till 2 and from around 7 to 10.30 p.m. Exact pub hours may vary from town to town. Children under 14 are not permitted in pubs, except where a special room has been set aside; alcohol is served only to adults aged 18 or older.

Cheese and Fruit

For the *last* course, if you can manage it, sample a selection of English cheeses: creamy Stilton, a blue-veined cheese; Cheddar, mild or sharp; Double Gloucester, a locally made yellow cheese, rich in flavour but rather dry; Caerphilly, from Wales, a fairly creamy variety; and Derby, mild and creamy. Cheese is usually eaten with biscuits (crackers), which often have a somewhat sweet taste, rather than with bread.

With your cheese, have port, or a piece of fresh fruit from the Vale of Evesham in the western Cotswolds. Cox apples

have more tang and flavour than Delicious, though both go well with cheese. Pears, plums, red and black currants, greengages (green plums) and strawberries are all grown locally.

Drinks

Sherry from Spain or Cyprus is the most common aperitif, followed by Campari or Pernod. Gin and tonic is very British, and very cooling in summer. If you ask for whisky, you'll be given Scotch, unless you specify Irish. Blended Canadian is sometimes available, bourbon less so.

A few brave vintners in Worcestershire and Gloucestershire produce English wines, but quantities are small; most restaurants offer a varied selection of imported wines. However, taxes on imported wine are high. You might have to settle for a fairly ordinary wine of rather undefined provenance though there are plenty of excellent ones around—at a price! Teetotalers can always drink tap water with meals; some restaurants serve Evian, Vichy and Perrier, plus Malvern water.

For centuries before large-scale trade brought wine to their tables, Englishmen drank only beer. A subject of intense national pride, English beers are perhaps the world's best—once you've acquired the taste. Don't compare a pint of stout or bitter to your usual beer. Rather, start thinking anew.

To the English, beer is a delicate and living substance which must be handled with care. First of all, it shouldn't be pasteurized or sterilized; the yeast must still be active when it's drunk. Nor should it be cold, but just slightly cool. Finally, it mustn't be pressurized or carbonated, but raised from the keg by means of a pump—gently.

The standard English beer is bitter, a caramel-coloured, naturally carbonated brew. Mild, which is reddish in colour, tastes somewhat sweeter than bitter; mild and bitter is a mixture of the two. Porter is darker and heavier, and stout, heavier still, due to its high hop content.

Ale is much like beer, but brewed at a higher temperature with more rapid fermentation. Lager resembles American and European beers. For a winter warmer, try barley wine, a kind of dark ale with the barley-malt base used in all beers. Take only a small amount, as this is stronger than it seems at first sip.

Pubs and Inns in the Heart of England

There are so many famous old pubs and inns in the area that it's impossible to list them all. Here is an arbitrary selection of establishments with particularly notable historical associations, pleasant décor or attractive settings—as well as wholesome food and drink!

Oxford

The Turf. Off Holywell Street in Bath Place. This popular pub in the vicinity of New College has pleasant small outdoor terraces.

Eagle and Child. St. Giles Street. The novelist and essayist C.S. Lewis and his friends gathered here during their years in Oxford.

The Bear. Blue Boar Street. Boasts an exhaustive collection of old school and rowing ties.

Golden Cross. Off Cornmarket Street. Tudor wall paintings decorate this historic pub, where it's claimed Shakespeare put on plays.

The Trout. Wolvercote. Thames-side pub, near the ruins of Godstone Nunnery. Known for its associations with the Pre-Raphaelites, a 19th-century group of writers and artists who met as undergraduates at Oxford.

Oxford Area

Bear and Ragged Staff. Cumnor. Open fireplaces cheer this old inn.

The Bear. Woodstock, near Blenheim Palace. This 12th-century coaching inn is still going strong—original oak beams and all.

Stratford-upon-Avon

Dirty Duck. Waterside. The theatre crowd has a fondness for this famous pub, not far from the RST.

White Swan Hotel. Rother Street. Historic inn near Shakespeare's Birthplace.

Falstaff Hotel. Bridge Street. Open fireplace and Tudor aura.

Shakespeare Country

Woolpack Hotel. Market Place, Warwick. Centrally located coaching inn.

Old Washford Mill. Studley. Centuries-old inn; pleasant gardens.

The Cotswolds

Manor House Hotel. High Street, Moreton-in-Marsh. Enjoy authentic English fare in the gracious setting of an old manor house.

Lygon Arms. Broadway. Attractive inn with beautiful antiques.

George Hotel. Winchcombe. A charming inn, distinguished architecture.

BLUEPRINT for a Perfect Trip

How to Get There

Although the fares and conditions described below have all been carefully checked, it is advisable to consult a travel agent for the latest information.

From North America

BY AIR: There are frequent non-stop flights (daily in many cases) to London from over 20 cities in the U.S. and Canada.

A number of reduced-price fares are offered. The APEX (Advance Purchase Excursion) fare must be reserved and paid for 30 days before departure and is valid for a trip of 7 to 180 days. One stopover is permitted for an additional charge. There is a penalty fee if you cancel. Super-APEX must be reserved 21 days in advance and is good for a period of 7 to 180 days, though no stopovers are allowed and your money is not refunded in case of cancellation. You book Standby fare the day you fly.

From Australia, New Zealand and South Africa

The APEX (Advance Purchase Excursion) fare is offered from Australia for a one-year maximum stay (no minimum stay requirement). This fare is also available from New Zealand (valid 21 to 180 days). There is a Return Excursion fare valid for a 21-day minimum to 270-day maximum stay for Australia and 21 days to one year for New Zealand. South Africa also has an APEX fare, valid 14 to 90 days.

From Eire

There are APEX (Advance Purchase Excursion) fares and a 6–30 day Excursion ticket. You can take the ferry and train to London, although the trip is almost as expensive as flying.

From London to Oxford, Stratford and the Cotswolds

If your flight lands at London's Heathrow or Gatwick, direct airport bus X70 leaves for Oxford several times each day. Flightlink Express coaches to Warwick also call at the airport.

A number of London-based tour operators offer excursions of one or more days to Oxford and Shakespeare Country. Or you can hire a car and drive yourself. Here's how you can go:

BY CAR

Oxford: The M40 will take you there directly.

Stratford: Best route is the M40 to Oxford, then the A34.

Cheltenham: Take the M40 and A40.

Moreton: Shortest drive is the M40 to Oxford, then the A34 to Chipping Norton, continuing via the A44.

BY RAIL

Oxford: Hourly departures from Paddington Station. Trip takes a bit over an hour.

Stratford: Euston Station to Coventry, changing to an express coach provided by British Rail. Actual travel time about two hours. Or Paddington Station to Leamington Spa, where you change for Stratford.

Cheltenham: Departures from Paddington; trip takes about 2½ hours.

Moreton: Frequent service from Paddington; travel time 1¾ hours.

BY COACH

Oxford: Departures every half hour from Victoria Coach Station; usually 1½ hours. Also frequent coach services from Heathrow and Gatwick.

Stratford: Service daily from Victoria Station; trip takes three hours.

Cheltenham: Four departures every day from Victoria Station; time three hours.

Moreton: Service daily leaving Victoria Station at noon. Travel time 2½ hours.

When to Go

May, June and September are perhaps the best months to visit the heart of England. Hotels, buses and trains won't be too crowded and the weather is quite pleasant, but if you do have to come in July or August, you'll at least get the warmest weather. Off-season visits (November to March) still hold many pleasures, including reduced rates.

Average monthly temperatures for the area:

		J	F	M	A	M	J	J	A	S	O	N	D
Max.	°F	45	46	50	55	63	68	71	70	66	59	50	46
	°C	7	8	10	13	17	20	22	21	19	15	10	8
Min.	°F	39	39	39	45	48	54	57	54	54	50	43	39
	°C	4	4	4	7	9	12	14	12	12	10	6	4

Planning Your Budget

To give you an idea of what to expect, here are some average prices in pounds sterling (£). However, due to inflation, they must be regarded as *approximate*.

Accommodation. *Hotels:* double room with bath and breakfast £30–80. *Guest houses* (without private bath): £20–30. *Bed & Breakfast houses* (without private bath): £15 and up.

Airport transfers. Heathrow to Central London, taxi £20, Underground £1.70. Gatwick to London Victoria, train £5.

Baby-sitters. £3–4 per hour during the day, evenings £3.

Bicycle hire. £4 per day for a 3-speed, £8 first week, £5 later weeks, £20 deposit.

Buses. Oxford 20p and up, Stratford 35p and up.

Camping. Tent or caravan (trailer) site £5–7 per night.

Car hire (international company). *Ford Escort* £22.50 per day plus 27p per mile, £154 per week with unlimited mileage. *Ford Granada 2.8 l.* £445.50 per week with unlimited mileage. Add 15% tax.

Coaches. London to Oxford £3 day return, to Stratford £8–11.

Entertainment. Cinema £2.50–4, discotheque, cabaret, nightclub £3.50–8, Royal Shakespeare Theatre performance £3.50–27.50.

Hairdressers. *Woman's* shampoo and set £6 and up, colour rinse £5–20, manicure from £2.50. *Man's* wash, cut and blow-dry £7–9, trim £2–6, shave £1–2.

Meals and drinks. English breakfast £5–6, Continental breakfast £3–4, pub lunch £2–5, 3-course dinner £6–15 and up, wine from £3.50 per bottle, beer (pint) £1, whisky 90p, soft drink 60p.

Museums, sights. 50p–£2.50, combination ticket to all Shakespeare landmarks £4.50 (child: £2).

Shopping bag. Loaf of bread 50p, 250 g. of butter 60p, 6 eggs 50p, 100 g. of instant coffee £1.80, half pound of fresh coffee £2.50, pint of milk 26p.

Taxis (Oxford). £1 for first mile, plus £1 for each additional mile. (Stratford) 80p for first half mile, 80p each additional mile.

Trains (2nd class day return). London to Oxford £8.40, to Stratford £11 and up. Oxford to Moreton £4.20.

An A–Z Summary of Practical Information and Facts

A star (*) following an entry indicates that relevant prices are to be found on page 103.

A

ACCOMMODATION*. England's hostelries range from palatial hotels situated in former manor houses and castles to very modest and inexpensive rooms in private homes. All must display details of prices, service charges and taxes. Breakfast may or may not be included in the price of the room. You often have a choice between the less expensive Continental breakfast (bread or rolls, fruit juice, coffee or tea) or a full English breakfast (see pp. 92–93).

Advance reservations are a necessity during the peak tourist season, especially in Stratford. For a small fee, the major Tourist Information Centres make advance bookings for all types of accommodation and any centre will help you find a room for the night. After office hours, a list of local establishments is displayed in front of most Tourist Centres. If you'd like to make your own arrangements, purchase one of the many British Tourist Authority guides to accommodation in Britain.

Hotels and motels. Unofficial ratings of some hotels are carried out by Britain's auto clubs, the Automobile Association (AA) and the Royal Automobile Club (RAC). A sign with the club's initials and one, two or three stars will be posted at the front of the hotel.

Registration is usually very informal, and you'll seldom be asked to pay in advance. Room prices are often quoted "b&b", that is, bed, breakfast, service and taxes per person. If the price is quoted per room, there will be a note to that effect. Rates vary widely, and many smaller hotels, though charming, can be surprisingly expensive.

Bed and Breakfast houses (B&B). Many households have one or two rooms to rent in their own homes. Apart from youth hostels, these are the most economical places to stay. Full English breakfast is always included in the price of the room, and you don't have to book in advance. Bed and breakfast houses are often situated in the same part of town, so if you drop by and one place is full, there's bound to be another down the road.

104

Guest houses. Guest houses are large private homes with about six bedrooms for rent. These are slightly more expensive than B & Bs, but usually cheaper than hotels. You probably won't find a bar, but there'll be a large, comfortable lounge with television. Breakfast is always included and, for an extra charge, the evening meal.

Farmhouses. Working farms in the heart of England often accept paying guests. Some offer just bed and breakfast, while others function along the lines of guest houses, with the option of taking an evening meal and the possibility of staying for long periods. Ask for the British Tourist Authority's pamphlet *Stay on a Farm: Where to Stay in England*.

Youth hostels. England's youth hostels are both good and inexpensive, but you may have to book far ahead to ensure yourself of a place during the busy season. Most hostels accept advance reservations. There are youth hostels in Oxford, Stratford (Alveston), Stow-on-the-Wold, Cleeve Hill, Charlbury and Cirencester (Duntisbourne Abbots).

For full information, write to:

Youth Hostels Association (England and Wales), Trevelyan House, St. Albans, Herts AL1 2DY

Or you can call at YHA Services Ltd.:

14, Southampton Street, London WC2E 7HY

You must present a membership card from your country's youth hostel association to use English hostels. If you don't have one, you can buy an International Guest Card at any hostel (available to anyone over five years of age). At most hostels, inexpensive breakfasts, box lunches and suppers can be purchased.

AIRPORTS*. London's Heathrow (principally for scheduled flights) and Gatwick (mainly charters) handle most passengers headed for the heart of England. Two smaller airports, Stansted and Luton, specialize in charter traffic. The closest major airport to Stratford is Birmingham International, served by scheduled domestic and European flights, and some charters.

Heathrow, one of the world's busiest airports, is located about 15 miles west of London. Several airlines run special bus services linking Heathrow with terminals in the city centre. If you're heading to the airport from the London area, be sure to check which terminal serves the airline you're travelling on.

The Piccadilly underground line to Heathrow provides a fast, inexpensive connection with all parts of London.

A   A railway line links Gatwick, to the south of London, with Victoria Station. Trains leave the airport buildings every 15 minutes during the day and take about 30 minutes to make the journey to Victoria Station.

If you want to go direct to Oxford from either Heathrow or Gatwick airports, without going into central London, there is a regular coach service, X70. The journey Heathrow–Oxford takes 65 minutes, Gatwick–Oxford, 130 minutes.

Facilities at Heathrow, Gatwick and Birmingham cover the full range: currency exchange offices (open 24 hours a day during the summer tourist season), car-hire counters, restaurants and bars, post offices and duty-free shops. There's a good supply of luggage trolleys and porters are always on hand should you need one.

Internal flights connect London's airports with Birmingham, but train and bus service to Oxford and Shakespeare Country is so comfortable and convenient (and less expensive) that ground transport is usually preferable.

B   **BABY-SITTERS*.** In the larger, more modern hotels, the staff may be able to look after small children by means of an intercom system. If the baby cries, the switchboard operator will dispatch a motherly staff member to look after him. Smaller hotels can always arrange for a local student to look after children; it's a good idea to make plans as far in advance as possible. Rates vary widely, but they're usually based on the sitter's age—the younger, the cheaper.

BICYCLE and MOPED HIRE*. Most shops which sell bicycles hire them out as well. To find the nearest one, look in the yellow pages under "Cycle Shops". If possible, you should reserve in advance during the months of July and August. Note that you can take bikes on many trains but reservations are required.

There are very few mopeds for hire, due to insurance difficulties and local protests about their noise and danger. You must be at least 16 years old and hold a moped permit to hire one.

For a full listing of shops that hire out bicycles and mopeds, plus information and suggested itineraries, ask for a copy of the British Tourist Authority's booklet *Britain on Two Wheels.*

BOAT HIRE and CRUISES. Whether you want to hire a narrowboat (a narrow houseboat which can navigate canals as well as rivers) or
book a room on a river cruiser, you should reserve in advance, espe-

cially for the July–August holiday period. You don't need a special permit to cruise the regional canals and rivers, though you must be at least 21 years of age to hire a narrowboat. The minimum hire period is normally one week. Narrowboats usually have from four to eight berths. If you wish to cruise the River Thames, the hire company can make the necessary arrangements if given at least four weeks' advance notice.

River cruises range from half-day tours with lunch or dinner included to several days aboard a hotel boat. The longer cruises allow ample time for sightseeing ashore.

Tourist Information Centres can direct you to local boat-hire and cruise agencies in Oxford, Stratford, Warwick and Rugby.

CAMPING*. Camping is a popular pastime in England. At present, there are nine campsites in the vicinity of Stratford and eight within easy reach of Oxford. Bus service links some of these campgrounds to nearby towns. If possible, reserve well in advance, as bookings are heavy during the busy months of July and August.

Campsites are usually equipped with showers, flush toilets, shaver points and other electric outlets. Gas cylinder refills are generally available. Most sites open only from March or April to September or October, though a few remain open year-round.

For complete lists of campsites and services in England, consult the British Tourist Authority brochure *Camping and Caravan Sites,* or write to:

Camping and Caravanning Club of Great Britain and Ireland, 11, Lower Grosvenor Place, London SW1V OEY; tel. (01) 828-1012

Tourist Information Centres will also provide you with a list of convenient camping places which accept tents and caravans (trailers). Many car hire companies rent out caravans and other large camping vehicles by the week.

CAR HIRE*. See also DRIVING. Both international and local firms operate in the Stratford/Oxford areas. The smaller businesses sometimes offer lower prices, but they may not provide convenient drop-off services or keep weekend hours. Enquire about the "Rail-Drive" scheme, in which you can pick up your car at principal railway stations in the region of Oxford or Stratford.

You must be at least 21, but not over 70, to rent a car in England. All you need is a valid driver's licence which you have held for at least 12 months. Unless you pay by credit card, you'll have to put down the

107

total estimated cost in advance, plus a deposit of up to £100. Some insurance coverage is included, but full (non-deductible) collision and personal accident insurance are charged per day. Drivers under 25 years old are required to purchase full collision insurance. Remember that 15% VAT will be added to the bill.

CIGARETTES, CIGARS, TOBACCO. The prices of tobacco products in Britain are proportionally among the highest in the world, and foreign brands are even more expensive. If you're a smoker, take full advantage of the tax-free allowance for visitors on your journey here (see CUSTOMS AND ENTRY REGULATIONS).

All the familiar international brands of cigarettes, cigars and cigarillos, plus domestic pipe tobacco (covering every taste from mild to strong) can be purchased at any tobacconist's.

Smoking is banned in some public places such as theatres.

CLOTHING. Nowadays, at dinner or the theatre, jacket-and-tie formality is rarely required. In summer you'll need a light raincoat for the occasional shower, and warm clothing for cool evenings. Spring and autumn can be surprisingly mild, but you should still be prepared with woollens and rain gear. Wintertime calls for heavy wools; temperatures indoors can be low and the dampness is penetrating. But you needn't pack a lot of warm clothing. British woollens, tweeds and sweaters are stylish and competitively priced.

Following is a comparison of British and American sizes. Remember however that clothing sizes may vary according to manufacturers. Men's suit and shirt sizes are the same in the U.S. and Britain.

Women's clothes					
Great Britain	10/32	12/34	14/36	16/38	18/40
U.S.A.	8/32	10/34	12/36	14/38	16/40
Women's footwear					
Great Britain	3	4	5	6	7
U.S.A.	4½	5½	6½	7½	8½
Men's footwear					
Great Britain	6	7	8	9	10
U.S.A.	6½	7½	8½	9½	10½

COMMUNICATIONS

Post office hours. Larger post offices are open: 9 a.m. to 5.30 p.m., Monday to Friday, from 9 a.m. to 12.30 p.m. on Saturday.

Oxford's main post office is a short distance from Carfax in St. Aldate's Street. The Stratford post office is in Bridge Street near the corner of Union and High Streets. Most Cotswold villages have post offices, though they sometimes double up as shops. Smaller town post offices and those in villages may close for an hour at lunch and on early closing day.

Stamps are sold at post office counters and from vending machines outside post offices. To post a letter, look for a bright red letter box, either the pillar type or a square box hung on a wall.

Poste restante (general delivery). If you don't know where you'll be staying, have your mail sent poste restante, in care of the post office in any town or village. No fee is charged when you call for your mail, but postal officials may want to see identification.

Telegrams no longer exist for messages within the U.K. They are replaced by Telemessages. Alternatively, use the post office services, Datapost, Expresspost and Intelpost. Enquire about details at the post office.

Telephone. Public coin telephones are situated in town centres. Bus and railway stations, hotels and some post offices also have public telephones. Old phones take 10p coins. The blue payphones, indicated by a blue or red telephone receiver symbol, operate with 2p, 10p and 50p coins. Payphones with one single slot also accept 5p, 20p and £1 coins. Cardphones have been introduced at strategic positions in airports, main railway stations, etc.

You can telephone most of the world direct from public telephones. For some countries, you'll still have to go through the operator and reverse the charges or pay with a credit card.

There are reductions for calling long distance from private phones between 6 p.m. and 8 a.m. for inland calls, from 8 p.m. for international calls, and all day Saturday and Sunday.

100	Operator
153	Directory enquiries for Europe and North America
010	International operator
192	Directory enquiries
999	For emergencies only: police, fire, ambulance

C **COMPLAINTS.** In Great Britain, there are laws to protect consumers. If an article doesn't correspond to its description, or is defective, you'll have no problem returning it provided you've kept the sales receipt. Though proprietors may offer you a voucher for the amount in question, you have the right to insist on a cash refund.

If you should have an unresolved problem with overcharging or bad workmanship, consult a local Citizens' Advice Bureau or the Consumers' Association:

14, Buckingham Street, London WC2N 6DS; tel. (01) 839-1222

In cases of gross abuse, go to the nearest police station.

CONSULATES. All embassies, consulates and Commonwealth high commissions are situated in London:

Australia: Australia House, Strand, London WC2B 4LA; tel. (01)379-4334; hours: 9 a.m. to 5 p.m. Monday to Friday.

Canada: Canada House, Trafalgar Square, London SW1Y 5BJ; tel. (01) 629-9492; hours: 9 a.m. to 5 p.m. Monday to Friday.

Eire: 17, Grosvenor Place, London SW1X 7HR; tel. (01) 235-2171; hours: 9.30 a.m. to 1 p.m. and 2.15 to 5 p.m. Monday to Friday.

New Zealand: New Zealand House, Haymarket, London SW1Y 4TQ; tel. (01) 930-8422; hours: 9 a.m. to 5 p.m. Monday to Friday.

South Africa: South Africa House, Trafalgar Square, London WC2N 5DP; tel. (01) 930-4488; hours: 9.30 a.m. to 4.30 p.m. Monday to Friday.

U.S.A.: 24, Grosvenor Square, London W1A 2JB; tel. (01) 499-9000; hours: 9 a.m. to 1 p.m. Monday to Friday.

CONVERTER CHARTS. England is slowly converting to the metric system. Draught beer and bottled milk are still sold by the Imperial pint, but most commodities are now measured in metric units. Temperatures are given in Celsius degrees, but length and distance, at present, are calculated in inches, feet, yards and miles.

Temperature

Length

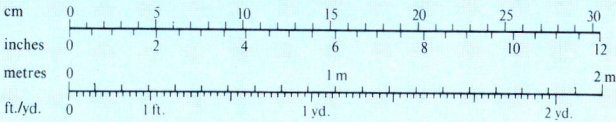

cm	0		5		10		15		20		25		30
inches	0		2		4		6		8		10		12
metres	0				1 m								2 m
ft./yd.	0		1 ft.			1 yd.					2 yd.		

Weight

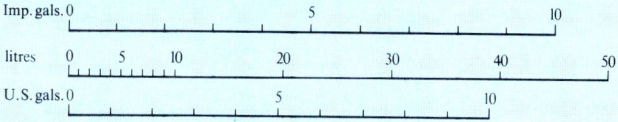

| grams | 0 | 100 | 200 | 300 | 400 | 500 | 600 | 700 | 800 | 900 | 1 kg |
| ounces | 0 | 4 | 8 | 12 | 1 lb | 20 | 24 | 28 | 2 lb. | | |

Fluid measures

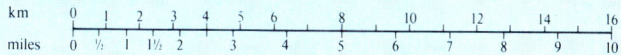

Imp. gals.	0				5					10
litres	0	5	10		20		30		40		50
U.S. gals.	0			5				10		

Distance

| km | 0 | 1 | 2 | 3 | 4 | 5 | 6 | | 8 | | 10 | | 12 | | 14 | | 16 |
| miles | 0 | ½ | 1 | 1½ | 2 | | 3 | | 4 | | 5 | | 6 | | 7 | | 8 | 9 | 10 |

CRIME and THEFT. Crime is hardly a problem in England's small cities and towns, but it's wise to take a few precautions. Remember that pickpockets frequent crowded places—markets, buses, shops. In bed and breakfast houses, lock your door as you would in a hotel—not against the management, but against your fellow guests.

CUSTOMS and ENTRY REGULATIONS. Citizens of the United States and Canada need only a valid passport for tourist visits, but nationals of most Commonwealth countries now require a visa. It's best to check in advance with your travel agent. Citizens of EEC countries can enter on a national identity card. However, careful checks are made on people entering for more than three weeks, e.g. amount of funds they carry with them, return tickets, etc., so entrants may have to face a barrage of questions. There are no passport controls between Eire and Britain.

Upon arrival in Great Britain you'll have to fill in an entry card with the address you'll be staying at during your visit. The immigration officer will stamp your passport, permitting you to stay in Britain for a specific length of time. Normally, stays are limited to six months. Pro-

C

111

C vided you look reasonably respectable and have sufficient funds with you, there's usually no problem.

Customs control consists of two channels. If you have goods to declare, take the red channel; otherwise follow the green route. Customs officers occasionally make spot-checks on green-channel travellers.

The following chart shows what main duty-free items you may take into Britain and, when returning home, into your own country:

Into:	Cigarettes		Cigars		Tobacco	Spirits		Wine
Britain*	400	or	100	or	500 g.	1 l.	and	2 l.
Australia	200	or	250 g. or		250 g.	1 l.	or	1 l.
Canada	200	and	50	and	900 g.	1.1 l.	or	1.1 l.
Eire	200	or	50	or	250 g.	1 l.	and	2 l.
N.Zealand	200	or	50	or	250 g.	1.1 l.	and	4.5 l.
S.Africa	400	and	50	and	250 g.	1 l.	and	2 l.
U.S.A.	200	and	100	and	**	1 l.	or	1 l.

* For non-European residents. (Eire: 200 cigarettes, 50 cigars, 250 g. tobacco.)
** a reasonable quantity.

Don't plan to bring a pet with you to Great Britain. All animals must be kept in quarantine for six months before they can enter the country.

Currency restrictions. There are no restrictions on the import or export of either British or foreign currencies. Check to see whether your own country has any regulations on the import and export of currency.

D **DRIVING in BRITAIN.** If you're bringing your own car to Britain, you'll need the registration papers and proof of full insurance coverage. The usual formula is the Green Card, an extension to your normal insurance making it valid in other countries. Almost all driving licences are accepted in Britain. The use of seat belts is mandatory; fines for not attaching them are high. Motorcycle drivers and passengers have to wear crash helmets.

Throughout the U.K., a driving licence is required, even for mopeds (motorbikes) under 55 cc. No one under 16 can operate a moped, 17 for motorcycles and scooters.

Roads and regulations. There are three important rules to observe when driving in Britain:

● Drive on the left

● Stop for pedestrians in "zebra" crossings (marked by broad black-and-white stripes and blinking amber lamps)

● Give way to traffic coming from the right, especially in roundabouts (traffic circles). Traffic already in the circle always has right of way.

It may take a few days for visitors from overseas to get used to driving on the left. Be on guard against your right-aiming instincts in emergency situations.

Roads in England are generally excellent. Most are two-lane, with no verge (shoulder), so you must look for lay-bys or parking areas if you want to stop for a rest. English drivers tend to go as fast as the road will reasonably allow. Speed limits, unless otherwise indicated, are 30 mph in towns, 60 mph on normal highways and 70 mph on motorways (expressways). Emergency phones are provided at regular intervals along motorways.

Parking. Never park on slanted white lines, which are for pedestrians only, or a double yellow line ("no waiting zone"). A single yellow line normally means "no parking", though you may park within the line at night and on Sunday.

The parking system in operation in Oxford city centre is "Pay and Display". Buy a ticket from the machine and place it in the window. It has on it your hour of arrival. Many smaller towns and villages, plagued with space problems during holiday periods, have established free car parks away from the centre of town. Signs will direct you to them.

As for pay parking, you may find meters, private car parks or lots with automatic ticket dispensers. To install your car in the latter, look for the ticket machine, insert the proper coin, and stick the ticket dispensed in the window of your car. Observe the time limit posted on signs.

In areas marked "permit holders only" or "tow-away zone", you're liable to have your car hauled away if you park.

Fuel and oil. Petrol (gasoline), formerly sold by the Imperial gallon (about 15% more than the U.S. gallon), is now dispensed by the litre in most areas. If you need help in calculating a conversion, see CON-

D VERTER CHARTS, p. 110. Octane grades are denoted by stars: two-star (92 octane), three-star (94 octane) and four-star (98 octane). Many pumps are self-service and some are coin-operated, allowing you to buy fuel 24 hours a day. Self-service stations usually have the lowest prices. No matter where you are, you'll have no trouble finding a petrol station. Attendants expect a small tip for any extra services rendered, but not just for pumping fuel.

Traffic police. Normally helpful and tolerant towards foreigners, traffic police can still be quite unsympathetic with speeders or drunken drivers (see below). Their vehicles may be anything from a Mini upwards, and often, but not always, are marked with a POLICE sign.

Drinking and driving. If you plan to drink more than a sip of whisky or half a pint of beer, you'd better leave the car behind. Penalties are severe, involving loss of licence, heavy fines and even prison sentences; and the law is strictly applied.

Breakdowns. Members of motor clubs affiliated with the British Automobile Association (AA) or the Royal Automobile Club (RAC) can take advantage of speedy, efficient assistance in case of a breakdown. Most European models can be serviced anywhere in England, but parts for American makes may have to be found in London.

AA: Fanum House, The Broadway, Stanmore, Middx HA7 4DF; tel. (01) 954-7373

RAC: Motoring Services Ltd., P.O. Box 100, RAC House, Lansdowne Rd., Croydon CR9 7JA; tel. (01) 681-3611

Road signs. Britain has adopted the same system of pictographs in use throughout Europe. *The Highway Code,* an official booklet available at most bookshops, contains a complete explanation of road usage and signs. Road maps usually carry definitions of signs as well. Some written signs may not be instantly comprehensible:

British	*American*
Carriageway	Roadway; traffic lane
Clearway	No parking along highway
Diversion	Detour
Dual carriageway	Divided highway
Level crossing	Railroad crossing
Moped	Motorbike
Motorway	Expressway
No overtaking	No passing
114 Roadworks	Men working

ELECTRIC CURRENT. The standard current in England is 240 volt, 50 cycle A.C. Most hotels have special sockets for shavers that operate on either 240 or 110 volts. England has a new three-prong safety plug; even if your appliance operates on the local current, you may need a plug adaptor.

EMERGENCIES. Help is as near as a telephone. Dial the emergency number 999 from any phone (no coin needed) for police, fire brigade or an ambulance.

Oxford, Stratford, Cheltenham, Cirencester and Moreton-in-Marsh all have sizable hospitals. In an emergency, hospitals and doctors affiliated with the National Health Service will provide foreign visitors with free medical care.

See also individual entries, such as CONSULATES, POLICE, etc.

GUIDES and TOURS. Many guided tours of Oxford and Shakespeare Country depart from London by train or coach. Whether you want to tour for a day or a month, any travel agent should be able to help you plan an itinerary. Qualified guides show visitors around at some major attractions and museums as part of the admission fee.

For a personally conducted tour, contact any of the local Tourist Information Centres. In the summer, a two-hour guided walking tour of Oxford leaves the local Information Centre several times each day.

HAIRDRESSERS*. England has its share of unisex salons. Prices are higher than in the traditional shops, but the finished product often has more flair, and certainly involves more pampering. If you'd prefer a simple cut in a less lavish establishment, look down side streets or above shops for small signs announcing "Gentlemen's Hairdresser" or "Ladies' Hairdresser".

It's customary to tip about 10% to the cutter and half that to the assistant.

HITCH-HIKING. It's legal, relatively safe and a popular means of transport for young people in summer. Hitch-hikers are not permitted to solicit rides on motorways (expressways). You can position yourself on an approach road to a motorway, but stay off the highway itself, where you are liable to a fine.

H **HOURS.** For post office opening hours, see under COMMUNICATIONS. Shops in Oxford and Shakespeare Country (except the largest ones) often close early at least one day a week.

Banks. 9.30 a.m.–3.30 p.m. Monday to Friday, and, in some cases, 9.30–12 noon Saturday.

Shops and stores. About 9 a.m.–5.30 p.m. Monday to Saturday. On early closing day, the smaller shops shut by 1 p.m. Tobacconists and newsagents open on Sunday to sell the morning newspapers and the odd groceries.

Tourist Information Centres. 9 a.m.–5 p.m. Monday to Friday. In small towns there may be an hour's break for lunch. In Oxford and Stratford, Information Centres have longer hours. They also open on Saturday, plus Sunday afternoon in summer (all year round in Oxford).

Stately homes and local museums. Most stately homes and museums in the country can be visited only from April to October. In April and October they open at weekends, increasing to five or six days a week from May to September. Many close for about an hour at lunchtime.

Stratford area sightseeing

Anne Hathaway's Cottage. November to March: 9 a.m.–4.30 p.m. Monday to Saturday, afternoon only on Sunday. April to October: 9 a.m.–6 p.m. Monday to Saturday (Sunday from 10 a.m.).

Birthplace. Same hours as Anne Hathaway's Cottage.

Hall's Croft. November to March: 9 a.m.–4.30 p.m. Monday to Saturday (closed Sunday). April to October: 9 a.m.–6 p.m. Monday to Saturday, 10 a.m.–6 p.m. Sunday.

Mary Arden's House. Same hours as Hall's Croft.

New Place. Same hours as Hall's Croft.

Royal Shakespeare Theatre. Evening performances 7.30 p.m., matinees 1.30 or 2 p.m.

Oxford sightseeing

All Souls College. 2–5 p.m. daily.

Ashmolean Museum. 10 a.m.–4 p.m. Tuesday to Saturday, 2–4 p.m. Sunday.

Balliol College. 10 a.m.–6 p.m. daily.

Bodleian Library. 9 a.m.–5 p.m. Monday to Friday, 9 a.m.–12.30 p.m. Saturday, closed Sunday.

Brasenose College. 10 a.m.–6 p.m. daily.

Christ Church. 9 a.m.–5 p.m. daily, Sunday 1–5 p.m. Picture Gallery: 2–4.30 p.m. daily.

Magdalen College. 2–6.15 p.m. daily.

Merton College. 2–5 p.m. weekdays, 10 a.m.–5 p.m. Saturday and Sunday.

Museum of Oxford. 10 a.m.–5 p.m. Tuesday to Saturday.

New College. 2–5 p.m. daily in term, 11 a.m.–5 p.m. during vacation.

Oriel College. 2–5 p.m. daily.

Queen's College. 2–5 p.m. daily.

St. John's College. 1–5 p.m. daily.

Sheldonian Theatre. 10 a.m.12.45 p.m. and 2–4.45 p.m. daily.

The Oxford Story, multi-media museum. 9 a.m.–7 p.m. in season (till 5–30 p.m. November to March).

LANGUAGE. Even if you're an English-speaking foreigner, you'll have to watch out for a few British peculiarities in pronunciation. Some words, especially place names, go back so many centuries that what you'll see in writing only slightly resembles what you actually hear. Gloucester, Worcester and Derby are pronounced as if they were "Gloster", "Wooster" and "Darby". Some Oxonians will tell you their college is "maudlin", but no criticism is intended—they attend Magdalen College. The River Cherwell comes out "Charwell" and Lord Leicester is called "Lester".

Quite apart from pronunciation problems, even beautifully enunciated words may mean something quite different from what you'd expect. Transatlantic differences, for instance, are so numerous that many bilingual (British-American) dictionaries have been published. To "ring off" is to end a telephone call, a long distance call is a "trunk call", the main street is always the "high street", and so on. Here is a mini-guide to transatlantic usage (see also under DRIVING IN BRITAIN):

British	American	British	American
bill	check (restaurant)	**first floor**	second floor
		ground floor	first floor
biscuits	cookies	**lay-by**	roadside parking spot
bonnet	hood (of car)		
boot	trunk (of car)	**lift**	elevator
caravan	trailer	**lorry**	truck
chemist	druggist	**off-licence**	liquor store

L

pants	shorts (underwear)	**tube or underground**	subway
pavement	sidewalk	**perambulator or pram**	baby carriage
return	round-trip (ticket)	**public school**	private school
single	one-way (ticket)	**push-chair**	baby stroller
subway	underpass	**to queue**	to stand in line
surgery	doctor or dentist's office	**(taxi) rank**	taxi stand

LAUNDRY and DRY-CLEANING. All towns and some villages have efficient laundries and dry-cleaners, as well as coin-operated establishments. Many hotels accept laundry, but you'll save money and time by taking clothes to the cleaners yourself. If you don't care to wait while the machines whirl, launderettes often do a "service wash" for an additional fee, meaning you leave your laundry and pick it up within a few hours washed, dried and often folded (but not ironed). Some dry-cleaners offer an express service, which usually takes less than a day, at an extra charge.

LOST and FOUND PROPERTY. Check with officials at the relevant train or bus station, or at your hotel. Report any major loss to the nearest police station; unless you do, and demand a certificate while you're at it, your insurance company at home may not pay up.

International Travellers' Aid helps arriving foreign visitors who've lost their money, passport, luggage, etc., and will also try to solve other problems. The office (open every afternoon and evening except on Christmas Day) is located in London at:

Victoria Station, platform 10, tel. (01) 834-3925

M

MAPS. You can pick up basic local maps and street plans at any Tourist Information Centre. If you're driving, ask at the same time for a copy of *Britain: A Map for Motorists.* This publication includes a map showing car ferry routes, motorways and other main roads, plus practical information for anyone touring by car. Bookshops, larger garages and some tobacconists carry a range of detailed maps.

HMSO (Her Majesty's Stationery Office) issue a full range of maps covering the entire country. Known as the Ordnance Survey maps, they come drawn to various scales in several series, down to 1:25,000. These are the best for hikers. As local bookshops frequently run out of smaller scale maps, you may want to pick them up in London.

MEDICAL CARE. Under Britain's National Health Service (NHS), foreigners can receive free emergency medical attention. Citizens of non-EEC countries are charged for routine appointments. Tourist Information Centres have lists of local doctors, dentists and hospitals. The National Health is supplemented by private doctors and hospitals. In England, the out-patient of a hospital is called the "Casualty Department". See also EMERGENCIES.

Chemist's. Every large town has a rotation system whereby at least one chemist's (like an American drugstore) stays open until about 8 p.m. and thereafter on call. Look in the local newspaper or the window of any chemist's for the name and number of the shop on 24-hour duty.

MEETING PEOPLE. There is no better place in England to meet old friends and make new acquaintances than in a pub; they're generally friendly, open places. Whatever your interests, you're likely to find someone to talk to after you've got your pint, glass of wine or soft drink.

Away from pubs, the English preserve more of their traditional reserve, but underneath they remain basically easy-going and good-natured. The best policy is to make the first move, break the ice, chat, smile and find some opening gambit. Then, and only then, will the Englishman open up—and you may have trouble stopping him. But brashness in all its forms, excessive noise or showing off, are not much appreciated.

Try to find out a person's name and use the formal address—"Mr. Smith" or "Mrs. Jones"; even if you're middle-aged or older, you'll drop very quickly into Christian name terms. And if you don't know a person's name, start the conversation with "Excuse me".

Among young people, attitudes are much more relaxed. Making friends—in pubs or shops or even in the street—is no problem; you'll be on a first-name basis straight away.

MONEY MATTERS

Currency. Since 1971, Britain has used a decimal currency based on the pound sterling (£). The pound is divided into 100 new pence (p).
   Coins: 1p. 2p, 5p, 10p, 20p, 50p, £1
   Banknotes: £5, £10, £20, £50
The pre-1971 1-shilling piece (equivalent in size and value to the new 5p piece) and the old 2-shilling coin (like the new 10p piece) still circulate.

M **Banks and currency exchange.** Banks give the best rate of exchange for foreign currency. Currency exchange bureaus can be found in shops and travel agencies. You won't get as good a rate here, and the fee charged for transactions may be quite high. Hotels change foreign notes and traveller's cheques for their guests. You always have to show your passport when changing traveller's cheques.

Traveller's cheques from the internationally known firms are readily accepted at many hotels, bed and breakfast houses, restaurants and shops. Cheques written against bank cards are cashable in many banks and other establishments.

Credit cards are accepted by many hotels (but not bed and breakfast houses), restaurants and shops. Signs are usually displayed indicating which cards can be used.

Value Added Tax. Since Britain is a member of the Common Market, practically all merchandise and services are subject to a sales tax (VAT) of 15%. Foreign visitors may escape this tax on certain conditions, but note that the scheme is operated only by certain large stores, small quality stores and specialist shops and, except in the case of large purchases, is hardly worth the trouble. Here's how to proceed: 1) have purchases shipped directly to your home address, or 2) ask the store to forward them to your port of embarkation (not applicable if you're leaving by air), or 3) take the goods with a detailed customs form from the store for presentation upon leaving the country; the tax will be refunded to you in due course. Visitors from EEC countries should present the form to their home customs, who will insert the local VAT rate for those goods. This form should be mailed back to the store where the purchase was made to obtain the refund. Quite a procedure!

Prices. See also TIPPING. Inflation and VAT (see above) keep English goods and services out of the bargain range. Hotel rooms and dining out are among the more expensive pleasures, followed by drinking and smoking (except for beer in a pub). But bed and breakfast houses offer very good value for money, and pub lunches are inexpensive, so you'll be able to splurge on your evening meal.

N **NEWSPAPERS and MAGAZINES.** Newsagents in Stratford, Oxford and the larger Cotswold towns carry a variety of publications, though the largest selection is on sale in Oxford. In fact, Oxford's choice of foreign newspapers and magazines is probably equal to or better than London's. American news magazines and the *International Herald Tribune* are widely available.

The *Oxford Mail* is published every day and the weekly *Oxford Times* comes out on Friday. A daily news-sheet of local happenings is posted in the Tourist Information Centre and some university buildings and pubs in term time; out of term it's issued weekly. You can buy the monthly *What's on in Oxford* at the Information Centre or from larger newsagents.

PHOTOGRAPHY. The golden glow of Cotswold stone buildings and the vivid green of the English countryside photograph well either in bright sun or in hazy weather. In fact, passing clouds may add dramatic shadows and highlights to a scene. But this is England, after all, and some days will be rainy and dark, requiring slower-speed film.

Standard brands and sizes of film are readily available at chemists' and souvenir shops, and sometimes at tobacconists and in department stores. Photo shops will develop your black-and-white pictures overnight, but most colour work is sent out. Allow about a week. Most shops that sell film can arrange for it to be developed.

Many historical buildings, including Oxford college halls and chapels, can be photographed, but you should always look for "No Photography" signs. Photography, with or without flash, is prohibited in theatres and concert halls.

Some outdated airport security machines, now rarely found, can spoil undeveloped film. If you're apprehensive, ask that your film be checked separately.

POLICE. Police in England's towns and villages are unarmed. They wear uniforms very similar to the ones made famous by London's "bobbies". As a general rule, policemen in cars wear peaked caps and those on foot patrol don the traditional helmets.

The principal duties of the traffic warden are to check parking meters and write tickets for violations. They sport a yellow-and-black checkered band around their caps.

You'll see fewer policemen on foot patrol in provincial cities, but if you need one in a hurry, go to any telephone and dial 999 (no coin required). Stratford's police headquarters is on the corner of Rother Street and Ely. You'll find the Oxford police station at the intersection of St. Aldate's Street and Floyd's Row.

P There are very few policemen patrolling the motorways in Britain, so if you plan on doing a lot of touring by car, you might want to join an automobile association (see DRIVING IN BRITAIN).

You should address a police officer as "Constable".

PUBLIC HOLIDAYS. There are eight public holidays throughout the year: New Year's Day, Good Friday, Easter Monday, May Day (first Monday in May), Spring Bank Holiday (last Monday in May), August Bank Holiday (last Monday in August), December 25 (Christmas Day) and December 26 (Boxing Day).

If one of these holidays falls on a Saturday or Sunday, the usual practice is to take it on the following Monday.

R **RADIO AND TV.** Two BBC (British Broadcasting Corporation) channels and two commercial, independent TV networks broadcast from early morning till about midnight.

On radio, five BBC stations provide news, music and feature shows for all tastes, from rock (BBC 1) to classics (BBC 3). Several commercial radio stations strongly challenge the corporation's ratings. The BBC World Service (648 KHz/463 m.) provides excellent international news coverage. If you're yearning to hear a voice from home, you can pick up the Voice of America, Radio Canada International and other shortwave transmissions.

Daily newspapers carry full radio and TV listings.

RELIGIOUS SERVICES. England's monarch is the spiritual head of the Church of England, which broke away from the Roman Catholic Church in the 16th century. Although Anglicanism is the country's official religion, freedom of worship is guaranteed. Tourist Information Centres keep lists of local places of worship, as do many hotels.

T **TIME DIFFERENCES.** England is on Greenwich Mean Time. In summer (between April and October) clocks are put forward one hour.

Summer time differences				
New York	**England**	Jo'burg	Sydney	Auckland
7 a.m.	**noon**	1 p.m.	9 p.m.	11 p.m.

TIPPING. Hotels and restaurants may add a service charge to your bill, in which case tipping is not really necessary. Otherwise, menus or bills specify "Service not included". You needn't tip in bed and breakfast houses. Cinema and theatre ushers do not expect tips. Likewise, barmen and barmaids in pubs are never tipped. See the chart below for further guidelines.

Hotel porter, per bag	minimum 50p
Hotel maid, per week	£5 (optional)
Waiter	10–15% (if service not included)
Taxi driver	10–15% (50p minimum)
Tour guide	10% (optional)
Hairdresser/Barber	10–15%, 4–5% to assistant

TOILETS. England is quite well supplied with public toilets. For some you may need a coin, but most are free. Look for signs at city street corners pointing the way to the Public Conveniences, Toilets, WC (for "water closet") or Lavatories.

TOURIST INFORMATION CENTRES. The British Tourist Authority has offices in various countries for your information before leaving home:

Australia Associated Midland House, 171 Clarence Street, Sydney, NSW 2000; tel. (612) 29-8627

Canada Suite 600, 94 Cumberland Street, Toronto, Ont. M5R 3N3; tel. (416) 961-8124

New Zealand Box 3655, 97 Taranaki Street, Wellington; tel. 55-3223

South Africa JBS Building, 7th floor, 107 Commissioner Street, Johannesburg 2001; tel. (011) 29-6791/29-6987

U.S.A. *BTA Headquarters:* 40 West 57th Street, New York, NY 10019; tel. (212) 581-47000
Regional offices: John Hancock Center, 875 North Michigan Avenue, Suite 3320, Chicago, IL 60611; tel. (312) 787-0490
Plaza of the Americas, North Tower, Suite 750, Lock Box 346, Dallas, TX 75201; tel. (214) 720-4040
612 South Flower Street, Los Angeles, CA 90017; tel. (213) 623-8196

T Throughout the rest of England, Tourist Information Centres listed by the English Tourist Board provide regional and local information, maps and reservation services. Following are addresses in the area covered by this book:

Banbury: The Museum, Marlborough Road off High Street; tel. (0295) 59855

Cheltenham Spa: 61, The Promenade; tel. (0242) 5228778

Cirencester: Cotswold Publicity Association, Corn Hall, Market Place; tel. (0285) 4180

Leamington Spa: The Southgate Lodge, Jephson Gardens, The Parade; tel. (0926) 311470

Moreton-in-Marsh: Council Offices, High Street; tel. (0608) 50881

Oxford: St. Aldate's Chambers, St. Aldate's Street; tel. (0865) 726871 (7 days a week), 726873 (accommodation)

Stratford: Judith Shakespeare House, 1 High Street at Bridge Street; tel. (0789) 293127

Warwick: Court House, Jury Street; tel. (0926) 492212

See under HOURS for information on opening times. Most smaller towns and villages post tourist information on a notice board near or inside one of the local government offices or in the town museum.

TRANSPORT

Buses and Coaches*. The British make a distinction between buses (which cover short rural or city routes) and coaches (for longer journeys). London Transport operate London's red double-deckers. Green Line buses serve the outskirts of London and the nearby countryside.

London's central coach station is the Victoria Coach Station, Elizabeth Street and Buckingham Palace Road. Don't confuse the coach station, for long-distance travel, with Victoria Bus Station for London's city buses. Coaches call at Heathrow and Gatwick airports and go to both Oxford and Stratford. City link X190 is a regular coach service from early morning to evening linking Oxford and central London (Marble Arch and Victoria Coach Station). City link X90 does 3 trips a day between London, Oxford, Woodstock and Stratford, with a stop at Blenheim Palace.

Oxford. The regional carrier is Oxford South Midland. The city's bus station is at Gloucester Green, a short walk from the railway station.

Stratford. The regional bus company is Midland Red with local service provided by Avonbus. Stratford's bus station is located in Warwick Road.

Cotswolds. In Cotswold towns and villages, schedules are posted in or near the local government offices in the centre of town. The bus stop is always within a few steps of the posted schedule. Though bus service may run daily between major towns, the smaller villages are served only on market days.

Always enquire about special bus and coach fares—if you're coming from abroad, you might be entitled to discounts not available to residents. Weekend Return tickets (half price for children) give discounted travel on certain lines from noon on Friday to noon Monday. Period return tickets, good for one return trip within three months, are always cheaper than two single (one-way) tickets.

Trains*. Paddington Station may not be an awe-inspiring sight, and the chaos, dirt and bustle might discourage you, but perseverance is worth it. Once on board, perhaps the most comfortable way to reach Oxford and Shakespeare Country is by train (see How to Get There, p. 100). British Rail trains are divided into first and standard-class cars. Unless you specify "first" (50% more expensive than second), you'll automatically be sold a standard-class ticket. Except for some commuter trains on the London–Oxford line, any train you take on weekdays will probably have a buffet car for snacks.

A bewildering array of special offers and passes makes buying your rail ticket a complicated business. For a quick trip, a Day Return or Weekend Return ticket is cheapest. If you plan to stay at your destination for several days, a Monthly Return ticket will save you money. Special rates apply in some cases for children, students and old age pensioners. Ask at a Rail Travel Centre for expert advice. Centres are located at Paddington Station in London and Oxford Station, and at Heathrow and Gatwick Airports. Travel agents can also provide information.

Before you leave home for Britain, ask your travel agent about the Britrail pass, which allows you unlimited train travel in Great Britain for a fixed time period at a flat rate. You must buy a Britrail pass before arriving in Britain. Once you arrive, however, there are still flat-rate, unlimited-use passes available, though not so all-encompassing as the Britrail pass. Enquire at a Rail Travel Centre for information on Runabout and Rail Rover passes.

Oxford Station has a restaurant-café, newsstand, car-hire telephone, Rail Travel Centre and left-luggage lockers. But other stations in the

T heart of England, including those at Stratford and Moreton, are very simple. Taxis meet trains at Oxford and Stratford, or you can take a city bus right outside the station which will carry you the short distance into the centre of town.

Taxis*. You may see a few black London-style taxicabs in the heart of England, but most cabs will be standard four-door models with the familiar illuminated "Taxi" sign on top. As walking is much more practical in Stratford and Oxford than in London, you won't see very many taxis. But a sufficient number dependably meet every train, and hotels will call a taxi by telephone for the return trip to the station. Taxi ranks are usually situated in town centres. In Oxford, taxis congregate in St. Giles, very near the Ashmolean Museum.

Taxis may or may not have meters. When there is no meter, the fee is determined by referring to an official list of rates. You may have to pay extra for luggage and for trips at night.

W **WATER.** Tap water is drinkable anywhere in England, though its high calcium content sometimes affects the taste. Bottled water is sold in some restaurants and in many grocers' and chemists' shops.

Index

An asterisk (*) next to a page number indicates a map reference. For index to Practical Information, see inside front cover.

Alcester 9*, 59*, 64
Architecture 42
Arden, Mary 58
Aylesbury 45

Banbury 9*, 45, 46
Batsford 67*, 69
Bibury 67*, 79
Bladon 9*, 44
Blenheim Palace 20, 40–41, 44–45
Bourton-on-the-Water 9*, 67*, 80, 90
Brass-rubbing 56, 73, 79
Broadway 9*, 67*, 71–72
Buckland 67*, 72

Chedworth Roman Villa 67*, 76–77
Cheltenham 9*, 76–77, 90
Chipping Campden 9*, 67*, 69–70, 90
Churchill, John, Duke of Marlborough 20, 40
Churchill, Winston 41, 44
Cirencester 9*, 77–78
Corinium Museum 77
Cotswold Farm Park 67*, 74
Cotswold Hills 9*, 66–81, 67*
Cotswold Wildlife Park 9*, 79
Curfew Tower · 68

Fairford 9*, 67*, 78–79
Food 92–99
Fosse Way 66, 76

Garrick, David 20, 51

Hundred Year's War 14, 15, 63

Lord Leycester Hospital 61–63
Lower Slaughter 67*, 81

Markets 82
Moreton-in-Marsh 9*, 23, 66–69, 67*, 81

Nightlife 89
Northleach 9*, 67*, 79

Oxford 9*, 24–39*, 25*
  Ashmolean Museum 25*, 38
  All Souls College 25*, 31–32
  Balliol College 25*, 29, 38
  Bodleian (library) 25*, 36–37
  Botanic Garden 25*, 35
  Brasenose College 25*, 27
  Broad Street 25*, 36, 81
  Carfax 24, 25*
  Christ Church (college) 25*, 26–27, 29, 39
  Christ Church Picture Gallery 27
  City Museum 24, 25*
  Corpus Christi College 25*, 33
  Divinity School 37–38
  Examination Schools 25*, 32
  Exeter College 25*, 38
  Hertford College 25*, 36
  High Street ("the High") 25*, 27, 31, 81
  Information Centre 24, 35*
  Magdalen College 25*, 33–35
  Merton College 25*, 29, 32
  New College 25*, 36
  Oriel College 25, 27, 29, 30
  Pembroke College 25*, 27

Queen's College   *25*, 32*
Radcliffe Camera   *25*, 31*
Sheldonian Theatre   *25*, 36*
St. Catherine's (college)   *35*
St. Edmund Hall   *25*, 29, 35–36*
St. John's College   *38*
Tom Tower   *24–26*
Town Hall   *24, 25**
University Church of St. Mary the Virgin   *25*, 30*
University College   *25*, 32*

Prices   *82*
Pubs   *89, 93, 96, 99*

Rollright Stones   *12, 67*, 69*

Shakespeare Country   *59*, 59–65*
Shakespeare, William   *48, 52, 55, 56, 59, 60, 63*
Shopping   *81–83*
Shottery   *58, 59**
Snowshill   *67*, 72*
Sports   *84–89*
Stately Homes
  Broughton Castle   *9*, 47*
  Buscot Park   *46–47*
  Charlecote Park   *59*, 60–61*
  Chastleton House   *67*, 69*
  Compton Wynyates   *9*, 45–46*
  Coughton Court   *59*, 64–65*
  Hinton Manor   *47*
  Kingston House   *47*
  Ragley Hall   *59*, 64*
  Rousham Park   *9*, 47*
  Sezincote   *67*, 69*
  Snowshill Manor   *67*, 72*
  Sudeley Castle   *67*, 74*
  Sulgrave Manor   *45*
  Waddesdon Manor   *45*

Stow-on-the-Wold   *9*, 67*, 81, 90, 91*
Stratford-upon-Avon   *9*, 48–59, 49*, 90, 91*
  Almshouses   *49*, 52*
  Anne Hathaway's Cottage (Shottery)   *58, 59**
  Avonbank Garden   *49*, 56*
  Bancroft Gardens   *49*, 57*
  Chapel of the Guild of the Holy Cross   *49*, 52*
  Garrick Inn   *49*, 50*
  Gower Memorial   *49*, 57*
  Great Garden   *49*, 52*
  Guildhall (Grammar School)   *49*, 52*
  Hall's Croft   *49*, 54*
  Harvard House   *49*, 50*
  Holy Trinity Church   *49*, 56*
  Judith Shakespeare House (Tourist Information Centre)   *49*, 50*
  Mary Arden's House (Wilmcote)   *58–59, 59**
  New Place Museum   *52*
  Royal Shakespeare Theatre   *49*, 56–57, 89*
  Shakespeare's Birthplace   *48, 49**
  Shakespeare Centre   *48, 49**
Sulgrave   *9*, 20, 45*

Upper Slaughter   *67*, 81*

Warwick   *9*, 59*, 61–64*
Warwick Castle   *63–64*
Wilmcote   *58, 59**
Winchcombe   *9*, 67*, 74*
Woodstock   *9*, 40, 44, 81*
Wool Churches   *66, 69, 77–78, 79*
Woolstaplers' Hall   *69*